Stanley Thor[nes]

PRIMARY

MATHS

Speaking and Listening Maths

YEAR

R–2

Wendy Clemson

Acknowledgements: A & C Black for 'The Appleman', 'Counting Steps', 'Here comes the bus', Crocodile' and 'Black Friars' songs in *Count Me In: 44 Songs and Rhymes about Numbers* (A & C Black, London, 1984) Penguin for 'Little Miss Muffet' and 'This is the House that Jack Built' in *The Puffin Book of Nursery Rhymes* (Opie, Penguin, Harmondsworth, 1963).

First published by
Stanley Thornes Publishers Ltd
Ellenborough House
Wellington Street
Cheltenham
GL50 1YW

99 00 01 02 03 \ 10 9 8 7 6 5 4 3 2 1

A catalogue record for this book is available from the British Library.

ISBN 0-7487-4910-1

Design by STP. Typeset by Tech Set Limited, Gateshead, Tyne & Wear.
Printed in Great Britain by Ashford Colour Press, Gosport, Hampshire.

Contents

INTRODUCTION

Oral and mental maths plays a key role in numeracy and this has been emphasised in recent national initiatives regarding mathematics. The National Numeracy Strategy highlights the importance of daily whole class work 'to rehearse, sharpen and develop mental and oral skills'. The activities in this book involve mental arithmetic and mathematical thinking; they can be used during these daily oral and mental sessions. However, the activities are intended to be flexible enough to be carried out during the first five or ten minutes of a lesson, or worked on for longer periods. All the activities are appropriate for use in a whole class context, and many can also be used with groups or individual children. The activities highlight key questions, for example 'How did you work that out?' and 'Who did it another way?'

Learning objectives are stated for each activity, and these match the year-by-year expectations identified by the QCA's *Teaching Mental Calculation Strategies* (1999) and in the *Framework for Teaching Mathematics* (1999).

This book comprises activities for use in Reception, Year 1 and Year 2. Teachers can choose, from any of the units, those activities that are appropriate for the children in each class. Within each unit the activities are not placed in order of difficulty, or with regard to the complexity of the maths involved. In any case, the concepts that particular children find easy or difficult will vary. Children will be at different stages in their understanding of number and differ according to the number facts they have committed to memory, and this may affect the strategies they use for mental calculations. Many activities include **Support** options to offer further consolidation and practice to help children progress and **Extension** options to challenge the children. These activities can therefore be set for appropriate individuals and groups across different year groups.

All the activities are starting points to enable teachers to adapt and devise their own bank of activities for their classes. A record sheet on pages 92–95 allows the teacher to keep track of the dates when an activity has been used to introduce or practise a particular mental calculation, concept or skill or to extend a skill, building on previous lessons or activities.

Some of the activities in this book use materials, for example, number cards and number lines, which can be found in the Stanley Thornes Primary Maths *Resources* files for Reception, Year 1 and Year 2.

Mental maths is important to the other maths work that children do. Mental calculation methods enable children to develop quick, efficient methods to use when working on written calculations, thereby enhancing their confidence with numbers. In addition, the title of this 'Speaking and Listening' book suggests an important link with these sessions to the National Curriculum for English. Throughout these activities, children will be:

- 'exploring, developing and clarifying ideas'
- 'making simple, clear explanations and choices'
- 'taught to listen carefully and to show understanding of what they see and hear by making relevant comments'.

All of these aspects of 'Speaking and Listening' are embedded within the daily oral and mental sessions. Additionally, the structured approach to the introduction of appropriate mathematical vocabulary, which is a feature of the *Framework for Teaching Mathematics*, is also incorporated within these activities. In other words, *Speaking and Listening Maths* can contribute to children's wider education as well as meeting the needs of the daily mathematics lesson.

Activity *Five alive*

LEARNING OBJECTIVES

Say and use the number names from one to five in order in familiar contexts *such as number rhymes …*
Count reliably in other contexts, such as clapping sounds or hopping movements
Begin to recognise 'none' and 'zero' in stories, rhymes and when counting

Resources

- *Shakers, maracas or other musical instruments*

Watch Points

Repeat the whole rap many times so that the children become quicker at counting.

If the children are not yet familiar with 'zero' adjust the rap to leave it out. If you include 'zero', highlight its importance when learning the rap.

After you have used this activity a few times, instead of saying the numbers at the start of each line, simply point to the numbers on the class number line and let the children say them all for you.

- With the children's help make up a class 'rap' involving the numbers zero to five. Use shakers, maracas or other instruments to 'count' out the numbers.

  Actions could be as follows:

  0 Begin by standing still with arms above head and fingers touching
  1 Punch one arm in the air
  2 Punch the other arm in the air
  3 Stamp one foot
  4 Stamp the other foot
  5 Nod the head

- Add another line or two while repeating the actions, for example:

  We know all our numbers
  We are the number wonders.

Activity *Dice dots*

LEARNING OBJECTIVE

Say and use the number names from one to five in order in familiar contexts *such as number rhymes, songs …*

Resources

- *A soft giant floor dice; a copy of the 'Dice Song'. A taped version of the 'Dice Song' and a copy of the sheet music can be found in* ***Blueprints: Early Years Songs and Rhymes****, (Stanley Thornes, 1994).*

Watch Points

The children might also hold up their fingers to show which number they are up to when counting the dots.

- Throw the floor dice into a circle of children. Allow all the children to count the dots aloud. The child nearest to the dice then throws it again.
- The children can sing along to the 'Dice Song' each time the dice is thrown. The verse sung depends on the roll of the dice.

The Dice Song

We've got one dot on top of the dice,
Roll it over again.
When it stops, we'll count the dots,
Roll it over again.

How many dots have we got now?
Count together and see …

We've got three dots on top of the dice,
Roll it over again.

[Verse 2:] *We've got three dots on top of the dice …*

Activity *One to five*

LEARNING OBJECTIVE

Count reliably everyday objects (first to 5), giving just one number name to each object

- Hold up flashcards at random and ask the children to call out the number displayed. Allow children in turn to act as 'teacher' by choosing and holding up the cards.

- Then set out all the cards on a desk, face up. Ask two children at a time to stand at the desk. When you call out a number, they should both find cards depicting that number, and hold them up for the class to see.

Extension: use number and picture cards to ten in later sessions. Target individuals with these higher numbers to check progress.

Resources

- *Large number cards from 1 to 5; cards with pictures of toys, balls, crayons and similar objects (showing up to a total of five objects). STPM* ***Resources*** *for Reception and Year 1 includes number and picture cards that can be used in this activity.*

Watch Points

This activity can be replicated with individuals and small groups. You can use the children's responses during these whole class sessions to make an informal assessment of their progress.

Number cards are useful as they allow the whole class to take part in an activity. You could provide each child with a set of these cards for use in these sessions. Each set might be laminated and held together using string laces.

Activity *My numbers*

LEARNING OBJECTIVE

***Recognise numerals 1 to 9**, then 0 to 10*

- Hold up the cards, one at a time, and present the children with challenges, such as:

  Hands up if this card shows your age. What number is it?

  Who has a telephone number with this number in it?

- With each challenge check that the number on show is said aloud at least once, and ensure that the whole class takes part by asking the children to repeat it or to count up to it.

  Extension: repeat the activity using numbers to 15 or 20 in a range of different contexts, for example, the number the child's favourite footballer wears on his back, the number of the school bus.

  Support: repeat the activity using numbers just to 5.

Resources

- *Number cards (make these, or use number cards from STPM **Resources** Reception or Year 1). Include, for example, all the ages represented in the class, and any other numbers with which the children will be familiar.*

Watch Points

A variation can be played by laying out the numbers and inviting a child to find a number that 'belongs' to them. They should then hold it up to show the class before announcing the number, and why it is important. This activity also assesses children's abilities to recognise and use numerals to 10. If you wish the children to focus upon number names, include cards with 'one', 'two', 'three' … 'ten' on them.

Activity *Rhymes to five*

LEARNING OBJECTIVE

Recite the number names in order, continuing the count backwards from a given number

- As you sing a song or rhyme, the children should use their fingers to indicate the number of things being sung about. Or choose five children to act out the rhyme while the rest of the class chants the words.

- **Five fat sausages**

  Five fat sausages frying in the pan,
  (Show five fingers)

  Sizzle, sizzle, sizzle, one went bang!
  (Clap hands loudly)

  Four fat sausages ...

  No fat sausages frying in the pan,

  Sizzle, sizzle, sizzle, the pan went bang!

- Question the children as the rhyme goes along, for example:

  How many things do we sing about next?

  How many things are there now in the song?

  How many things have gone (bang)?

  How many things did we begin with?

  How many things would there be if they all came back?

Resources

- *A collection of rhymes and songs that involve counting back from five. Examples from* ***Blueprints: Early Years Songs and Rhymes*** *include: 'Five little teddy bears', 'Five little speckled frogs', 'Five currant buns in a baker's shop', 'Five little ducks went swimming'. STPM* ***Reception Teacher's Book*** *also includes many good examples of counting rhymes.*

Watch Points

The rhymes can be adapted to fit your circumstances. If, for example, the class has five pet goldfish, or there are five jam tarts in the 'class shop', the children can help work out rhymes to include these. The rhyme can then be added to the class and school repertoire.

Activity *Rockets*

LEARNING OBJECTIVES

Say and use the number names in order in familiar contexts such as number rhymes, songs ...
Recite the number names in order, continuing the count forwards or backwards from a given number
Count reliably up to 10 everyday objects *giving just one number name to each object*

- Ask ten children to crouch in a row at the front of the class. Tell them they are rockets ready for take-off. They should then jump up smartly in turn, as the remainder of the class counts them. This can be repeated several times, gradually increasing the speed of the count.

- Choose a child somewhere along the line and ask all the 'rockets' up to and including this child to stand up. Ask the class how many rockets have 'taken off'. Repeat this for differing number groups, including groups which do not include those children at the beginning of the line (for example, the first and second children).

- Ask the children to count down from ten, holding up the appropriate number of fingers as they count. As they say 'Lift-off!' or zero, they can throw their arms into the air.

Extension: repeat the rocket activity using 20 children, and 'launching the rockets' from different starting numbers.

Watch Points

'Launching the rockets' from different starting numbers will help to assess which children are able to count reliably to 10. Asking the children to, for example, 'count on three rockets to 9' will further consolidate this work.

Activity *Rhymes to ten*

LEARNING OBJECTIVE

Say and use the number names in order in familiar contexts such as number rhymes, songs …

- Teach the children a rhyme, and then split the class into two groups. One half sing the numbers, while the other half sing and do the actions. Then they can swop activities.

- **One, Two, Buckle My Shoe**

  One, two, buckle my shoe,
  Three, four, shut the door,
  Five, six, pick up sticks,
  Seven, eight, lay them straight,
  Nine, ten, a big fat hen.

Resources

- *Find some rhymes and songs that involve counting to ten. (See* ***Blueprints: Early Years Songs and Rhymes****.)*

Watch Points

Repeat these rhymes frequently throughout Reception and Year 1. At this stage, children enjoy hearing counting rhymes and songs that they know well. Singing and acting a version of 'One, two, buckle my shoe' will engage the children and will help to practise the order of the numbers to ten.

Activity: *One to twenty*

LEARNING OBJECTIVES

Say and use the number names in order in familiar contexts
Begin to recognise 'none' and 'zero' when counting
Read numerals to at least 20

Resources

- *A class number track from one to twenty; pieces of card that can be laid over the numerals*

1	2	3	4	5	6	7	8	9	10	11	12	13	14	15	16	17	18	19	20

- Ask the class to call out all the numbers in order, starting at one, while you point to the numerals. Then allow one or two volunteer children to do the pointing in turn, while the children call out the numbers again.
- Then point to numbers along the track at random and ask the whole class, or individual children, to name the numbers.
- When all the children can identify the numbers, mask some of the numbers, and ask individual children to say what number is 'missing'. At first these should be individual numbers, then two or three numbers can be masked together.

Support: repeat the activity using a number track from one to ten.

Watch Points

Note that the numbers on the track sit in spaces. This is not a number line, where the numbers must mark points on the line itself.

Activity *Ten to none*

LEARNING OBJECTIVE

Recite the number names in order, continuing the count backwards from a given number

- Ask the children to sit in a circle. Hand out the card sausages (for example) at random. As all the children sing the rhyme, those with cards should hold them up and then put them down as they 'drop out' of the rhyme.

- **Ten fat sausages**

  Ten fat sausages frying in the pan,
  (Show ten 'sausage cards')

  One went pop and another went bang!
  (Clap hands loudly)

  Eight fat sausages frying in the pan ...
  (Adjust number of 'sausage cards' held up in each verse)

  No fat sausages frying in the pan,
  Sizzle, sizzle, sizzle, the pan went bang!

Resources

- *Use counting rhymes and songs which specifically involve counting back from ten. Examples include: 'There were ten in the bed', 'Ten fat sausages', 'Ten green bottles', and 'One man went to mow'. Make card resources, such as ten pictures of fat sausages, to help the children enact the rhymes.*

Watch Points

In subsequent sessions, vary the number of cards handed out, so that the children are not always starting their counting back from ten. 'Ten fat sausages' can also be used to practise counting back in twos.

Activity *More or less*

LEARNING OBJECTIVES

Use language such as more or less, greater or smaller, to compare two numbers
Compare two given numbers and say which is more or less, *and say a number which lies between two given numbers*

Resources

- *Number cards from 0 to 20. Make these, or use enlarged number cards from STPM Year 1* ***Resources***.

- Hold up a card and ask the children what number it is. Then show another card and ask questions such as:

  This card says ten, now what number is on here? (Twelve)
  Is twelve a lower number than ten?
  Is twelve fewer than ten?
  Is twelve less than ten?
  Is twelve a bigger number than ten?
  Is twelve more than ten?

- Now put down the '12' card and take up another. Question the children again, asking them to compare the new number with the original '10' card. Then begin afresh with a different starting card.

  Extension: repeat the final activity asking the children to give a number that lies between the two cards selected.

Watch Points

In subsequent sessions, after the first card is shown, you might ask one child to select a card and show it to the class. If the first card is '8' and the child selects '5', the class should say in unison, 'Five is less than eight'. Repeat this game giving all the children several chances to choose a number.

Encourage the children to answer using complete sentences, for example, '12 is *greater than* 10'. This will help to reinforce their understanding of the appropriate mathematical vocabulary throughout this activity ('more', 'larger', 'bigger', 'greater', 'fewer', 'smaller', 'less').

The range of mathematical vocabulary used should be appropriate to the age of the children. The National Numeracy Strategy *Mathematical Vocabulary* book will help you to select the words and phrases that children in different year groups need to understand and use.

Activity *Ten smiling faces*

LEARNING OBJECTIVE

Count in tens

- Hold the card hands up as you would your own hands (palms outwards and thumbs almost touching).

- Ask the children how many 'smiling people' there are. Then allow them to hold up their own hands in the same way and call out 'ten'. Then ask them to squeeze the hands shut, and then pretend to show ten more people. Ask:

  How many people now?

  The children should say:

  Twenty people.

- The children should go on revealing their fingers in tens and counting in unison in tens up to and back from a hundred.

Support: repeat the activity counting in tens up to fifty.

Resources

- *Cut out two large hand shapes, one left and one right. Draw smiling faces at the top part of the fingers and thumbs.*

Watch Points

The STPM class number line or large 100 square might be used to point to the children's counts. Mark on the different steps as the children count.

Activity *Count in twos*

LEARNING OBJECTIVE

Count in twos

- Ask ten children to hold two objects each, one in each hand. The children can stand in front of the class, form part of a circle comprising all the children in the class or stay in their seats.

- Ask the class to count in twos, while each child holding the objects takes a turn at showing the 'two' which they are holding. The children can hold them behind their backs and produce the objects when their turn comes. At the end of the session the set of objects can be placed together, so that the children can see that all the twos make a total of twenty.

Support: you could ask the children to count in ones, but to say every other word in a whisper. This will help them to 'hear' the pattern of counting in twos.

Resources

- *Collections of objects which can be held in the hand, for example, Colour Factor© ten rods or crayons*

Activity 'Buzz' game

LEARNING OBJECTIVE

Count in twos

- Ask the children to sit in a circle. They should take turns to say the next number in sequence, starting at one, but numbers in the 'counting twos' pattern should be replaced by the word 'buzz'. For example:

  One, buzz, three, buzz, five, buzz...

Watch Points

Before they play this game the children should have had plenty of practice at counting in twos in different contexts. Number rhymes such as 'Ten fat sausages sizzling in the pan' or 'Ten little squirrels sat on a tree' (see *Blueprints: Early Years Songs and Rhymes*) offer suitable reinforcement. The 'buzz' game reinforces the pattern of numbers (for example, counting in twos involves counting 'every other number').

Activity Before and after

LEARNING OBJECTIVES

Recite the number names in order, counting on from a given number
Find one more or one less than a number
***Compare two given numbers** and say which is more or less, and say a number which lies between two given numbers*

Resources

- *Two bean bags of different colours*

Watch Points

If the children have not worked with 'zero', the game can still begin at one but the first child should say just 'one' and hand on the beanbag.

- Ask the children to sit in a circle. Give each child a number, starting at one and moving in sequence around the circle. Show the children one of the beanbags and say it is a 'what comes before?' beanbag. Give the beanbag to the child number one and ask the child to say 'one' and then the number which comes before it (zero). They then pass the beanbag on to child number two who should say 'two and before it comes one'. They then hand the bag on, until it has gone right around the circle.

- Take back the 'what comes before?' beanbag and show the children the other one. Explain that this is a 'what comes next?' beanbag. As they pass this around, each child says their own number and the number that comes next.

- Play the game again with both beanbags going around, one just behind the other.

  Extension: in subsequent sessions the game can be played using different number sequences, starting, for example, at 21, 43 or 50.

Activity *Who's first?*

LEARNING OBJECTIVES

Understand and use the vocabulary of comparing and ordering numbers
Begin to understand and use ordinal numbers in context

- Split the class into four groups and assign each a colour to match one of the card people. Place the card people in a 'queue' alongside the van. Ask the children who will have an ice-cream before the others. Point out that we say the person at the front of the queue is first. If the person at the front of the queue is, for example, wearing blue, the blue group should put up their hands and call out 'first'.

- Re-order the queue so that another group can call 'first'. Do this several times.

Extension: repeat the activity using up to ten card people so that children become familiar with ordinal numbers to 'tenth'.

Resources

- *Four card 'people' (each a different colour) and one ice-cream van, each with a card tab so that they will stand up. Plastic play figures could also be used.*

Watch Points

Variations might include: Who is *last* in the queue? Who is *last but one* in the queue?

Children should be familiar with 'first' and 'last' from practical work in Reception.

You might encourage the children to respond using whole sentences, for example, 'The blue person is first.' This will help to reinforce the vocabulary.

Activity *Champions*

LEARNING OBJECTIVES

Understand and use the vocabulary of comparing and ordering numbers

Begin to understand and use ordinal numbers in context

- Ask three volunteers to wear or hold up one of the runners, while standing in a row in front of the rest of the class. Tell the children that these people have been in a race. Point out that the person on the left (from the children's point of view) is the winner, with the other two coming in the next two places.
- Now ask questions such as:

  Who is first?

  What position is the next person in?

  Where is (child's name)?

  Who is before the third person?

- Then change the order of the children standing in the row, and repeat some of the questions.

Resources

- *Three card swimmers or runners. These can be tabards that the children put over their heads or card outline pictures that the children hold up.*

Watch Points

The activity can be done with another set of three children, to give those involved in the first session the chance to answer. You might also add more children to the 'race' and more questions: 'Who is fourth?' 'Who is between second and fourth?' 'Who is last?'

Activity *What comes next?*

LEARNING OBJECTIVES

Describe and extend number sequences
Make simple estimates and predictions

- Call out a number pattern and ask the children:

  What comes next?

  Here are some examples, with the patterns getting progressively more complex:

0, 1, 2, 3, 4	(counting numbers from 0)
46, 47, 48 ,49	(counting numbers starting from a number other than 0)
20, 19, 18	(counting back)
0, 2, 4, 6	(counting in 2s)
0, 10, 20, 30, 40	(counting in tens)
1, 2, 1, 2, 1	(two number repeat)
1, 2, 3, 5, 6, 7, 9, 10, 11	(3 numbers, omit one)

Extension: this activity will be particularly useful in Year 2 as 'describing and extending number sequences' is a 'key objective' at this stage. Children will be expected to create their own number patterns during 'Counting' lessons. These might be collected and used for subsequent 'What comes next?' number pattern sessions. Ask a child to explain each pattern as well as to extend it.

Activity *Tapping fives*

LEARNING OBJECTIVE

Count in steps of 5 from zero to 20 or more, then back again

- Ask the children to lay the flats of their hands on their tables. They can then tap out a rhythm, using both hands while chanting the pattern of fives. This is how it should go:

  0 – tap table with fists (fingers closed)
  5 – tap left hand once
  10 – tap right hand once
  15 – tap left hand twice
  20 – tap right hand twice

- When the children are skilled at this, ask them to tap the count down in fives (20, 15, 10 …).

Extension: in subsequent sessions the total to which the children count can be extended beyond twenty.

Watch Points

Show the class the pattern of fives using the class number line or 100 number square.

Activity *Counting up and down*

LEARNING OBJECTIVES

Know the number names and recite them in order to at least 20, from and back to zero
Count on or back in ones from any small number …

- Sit the children in a circle. Hand out the cards at random, so that each child has a card. Allow the children to hold up their cards, when their turn comes, while the class recites the numbers from zero. The pace of the reciting should enable each child to show their card to the rest of the class before moving on. Over several sessions the children should become quick at reciting the numbers and displaying their card appropriately.

- Once the children can do this count quickly, ask them to count down from the highest number available (which depends on the total number of children in the class) to zero.

Resources

- *Number cards from zero up to the total number of children in the class. STPM* ***Resources*** *Reception, Year 1 and Year 2 includes number cards to copy and cut out.*

Watch Points

This activity can be used with children in Reception and Year 1 and 2 to rehearse and sharpen their counting skills. The starting number for the counts can be varied according to the work already covered by the children.

Activity *On and back in tens*

LEARNING OBJECTIVE

Count on or back in ones from any given small number, and in tens from and back to zero

Resources

- *A small drawstring bag with ten marbles in it*

- Invite the children to sit in a circle. Give the bag of marbles to one child who begins the counting by saying 'ten'. The bag is then passed around while the whole class counts in tens, adding ten every time the bag changes hands. When 100 is reached the next child can start the counting back by saying '90'.

  Support: repeat the activity, counting in tens to and from 50.

  Extension: at the start of the count, ask the children to guess who will hold the bag when the count reaches a 100.

Watch Points

Repeat the game with children simply holding up their hands with ten fingers spread as they call out the count in tens.

Activity *Odds and evens*

LEARNING OBJECTIVE

Count on in twos from zero, then one, and begin to recognise odd and even numbers to about 20 as 'every other number'

Resources

- *Washable felt-tipped pens, or pens and card*

- Either ask the children to copy the word 'odd' onto the palm and the word 'even' on to the back of one hand. Or ask the children to write 'odd' on one side and 'even' on the other side of a piece of card.

- Start the children counting at zero, and then show them how to flip their hands or cards over and back, horizontally, so that as they count the words 'odd' and 'even' are revealed alternately.

- Stop the counting from time to time and ask questions such as:

  Is five odd or even?

  What is the number before five?

  Is that number odd or even?

  What is the number after five?

  Is that number odd or even?

Activity *What's in threes?*

LEARNING OBJECTIVE

Count in steps of 3 from zero

- Place three teddies on the desk saying:

  Here are the three bears.

  Then lift them up and place them down again saying:

  And another three is six bears.

  Continue up to 21.

  Extension: in subsequent sessions, the totals might be extended to 30 and beyond.

Resources

- *A collection of objects and pictures of things that come in threes, such as points on a triangle, legs on a stool, wheels on a tricycle, the three bears, three yoghurts in a pack*

Watch Points

'The Three Bears' story offers a popular context for maths work (for example, measures: 'height and size').

Activity *Numbers to 100*

LEARNING OBJECTIVE

Say the number names in order to at least 100, from and back to zero

- Invite the children to count out loud together starting from a different number in each session. Children can take it in turns finding the starter numbers. Ask questions such as these to get a range of starting numbers:

  When is your birthday?

  What is your house number?

  What is the date today?

  What is your favourite number?

- Alternatively, children in turn can select starting numbers by taking a number ball from the bucket.
- To practise counting back, ask a child to select a ball from the bucket (which should be held at head height so that the child cannot see the numbers). The class can then count back from this number to zero.

  Support: a large 100 square or class number line could be displayed to show children the sequence of numbers.

Resources

- *A bowl or basket with some table-tennis balls in it. Number the balls using a felt-tipped pen. If as suggested below, the balls are to be used for counting back, choose numbers between 50 and 100. (The balls can be washed and reused.)*

Watch Points

In some sessions, instead of counting the whole sequence of numbers, you might, for example, ask the children to 'Count on 20 from 46', 'Count back 5 from 95'.

Activity *Counting patterns*

LEARNING OBJECTIVE

Count on in steps of 3, 4 or 5 to at least 30, from and back to zero, then from and back to any given small number

- Give every child a card at random from the set. Allow all the children in the class to assemble in their number groups, with for example, all the '2s' together. Then invite each group in turn to count in steps of their number, with every child, in turn, calling out a number in the pattern.
- As an example, if there are 30 children in the class, and ten take a '2' card, eight a '3' card, six a '4' card and six a '5' card, their patterns of counting will extend like this:

  (0) 2, 4, 6, 8, 10, 12, 14, 16, 18, 20 (ten '2s')

  (0) 3, 6, 9, 12, 15, 18, 21, 24 (eight '3s')

  (0) 4, 8, 12, 16, 20, 24 (six '4s')

  (0) 5, 10, 15, 20, 25, 30 (six '5s')
- The cards can be returned and each child can take a different one so that the game can be played again.

Support: limit the 'target numbers' to about 20. You might also limit the use of sequences involving multiples of 4.

Resources

- *Sets of number cards: fifteen cards with a '2' on them, ten cards with a '3', seven cards with a '4' and six cards with a '5'*

Watch Points

Note that in different sessions children will have chances to be a member of each number group, and the number patterns to 30 will all be practised.

Activity *Twos and tens*

LEARNING OBJECTIVE

Begin to recognise two-digit multiples of 2, 5 or 10

- Choose which multiples are to be explored. In the following example the multiples of two are used. Display the 100 square where all the children can see it. Mask all the columns of numbers which are not in the counting pattern of twos (that is the columns headed by 1, 3, 5, 7, 9).

  Point to the numbers along the top row and allow the children to count them. Ask them what the pattern is, and they should recognise the counting pattern of twos. Then point along the first and second rows while they count.

  Then stand back from the 100 square and allow them to count in twos from the beginning to 100.

- In other sessions, ask a child to point out where the counting pattern of tens appears on the 100 square. (It fills the far right hand column only.) The children can count this pattern while a child points to the numbers. The children can then be reminded that the pattern of twos, as shown on the 100 square, has in it all the numbers in the pattern of tens.

Resources

- *A class-sized 100 square. Attach Blu-Tack© to five strips of card, so that entire columns of numbers can be masked. Make the 100 square, or use posters from STPM Year 1 or Year 2.*

Watch Points

If the children are working with fives, the columns headed 1, 2, 3, 4, 6, 7, 8 and 9 need to be masked. Use strips of card for this. Links can be made between the counting pattern of fives and tens.

Activity *Tens and units*

LEARNING OBJECTIVES

Begin to know what each digit in a two-digit number represents
Partition a 'teens' number and begin to partition larger two-digit numbers into tens and ones (TU)

- Give each child a number card. If space permits, take three (or four) children without cards and name them 'no tens', 'one ten' and 'two tens' (and 'three tens' if required). Ask the rest of the class to line up behind their appropriate 'ten' (for example, if they are 13, they should stand behind 'one ten', if they are 24 they should stand behind 'two tens'). Let them hold up their cards.

- Ask individual children questions and challenges to check that everyone is in the correct line. For example:

  Tell me why you joined the 'one ten' line.

  Show me the tens on your card.

  How many tens in your number?

- In subsequent sessions when the children can identify the 'tens' lines confidently, appoint leaders who are, for example 'two units or ones' or 'odd ones' or 'six units'. Invite the children to join the lines if their number fits, but to stay seated if it does not.

  Extension: repeat the activity with different number cards, this time going up to 'four tens' or above.

Resources

- *Number cards (one for each child in the class). The range of numbers can be changed from session to session – initially numbers to match the number of children in the class. Make these cards or use STPM Reception, Year 1 or Year 2* ***Resources***
- *Pieces of blank card of different colours*

Watch Points

If space is limited you could hold up coloured cards, and say, 'If you have no tens you are in green group. If you have one ten you are in red group …' and so on. Then hold up the coloured cards again, one at a time, in random order. The children then hold up their card when their group colour shows.

Activity *One more, ten more*

LEARNING OBJECTIVE

Say the number that is 1 or 10 more or less than any given number to 20 or more

- Ask the children to get into pairs. Give each pair a number. Over the first few sessions these can be the counting numbers from one (for adding one and ten only) and then from ten (to allow counting on and back). Go around the pairs. The children should do the following:

  – Announce their number.
  – Say what the number and one more than the number is.
  – Say what the number and ten more than the number is.

  Also, if appropriate:
  – Say what the number and one less than the number is.
  – Say what the number and ten less than the number is.

  Extension: repeat the activity using numbers up to 100 or above.

Resources

- *Coins up to 20p (optional)*

Watch Points

This exercise might be repeated using the context of money, with the children saying what is 1p or 10p more or less than a given amount.

Activity *More or less*

LEARNING OBJECTIVE

Compare two given two-digit numbers, say which is more or less, and give a number which lies between them

- Sit the children in a circle. Give each child a number card and choose a child to start. Say a number (for example, 20). The child starting has to say whether their number is more or less than your number, then offer a number that is in between the two numbers, for example:

  31 is more than 20. 25 lies in between 31 and 20.

- The next child then compares this 'in between' number with his/her own, and the game continues.

- This activity should be played right around the circle, more than once if time allows.

Resources

- *Number cards from 2 to 99*

Watch Points

You might play a version of this game using money or measurements by making cards with appropriate values, for example, 50p or 50 cm.

Activity Ordinal numbers to twelve

LEARNING OBJECTIVE

Understand and use the vocabulary of comparing and ordering numbers, *including ordinal numbers*

- Teach the children the 'Black Friars' song:

Seven Black Friars,
Sitting back-to-back,
Fished from the bridge
For a pike or jack.
The first caught a tiddler,
The second caught a crab,
The third caught a winkle,
The fourth caught a dab,
The fifth caught a tadpole,
The sixth caught an eel,
And the seventh one caught an old cart-wheel!

- Show the children pictures of the creatures in the song (a jack is a young pike). Then quiz them using questions such as:

What did the first friar catch?
Which friar came after the second one?
Who caught the tadpole?

- If Christmas is approaching, repeat using 'The Twelve Days of Christmas'. The last verse is as follows:

On the twelfth day of Christmas, my true love gave to me:
Twelve drummers drumming,
Eleven pipers piping,
Ten lords a-leaping,
Nine ladies dancing,
Eight maids a-milking,
Seven swans a-swimming,
Six geese a-laying,
Five golden rings,
Four calling birds,
Three French hens,
Two turtle doves,
And a partridge in a pear tree.

Ask questions such as:

What happened on the first day of Christmas?
When was I given seven swans?

Resources

- *Copies of 'Black Friars' (from* ***Count Me In: 44 Songs and Rhymes about Numbers****) and 'The Twelve Days of Christmas'*

Watch Points

Songs and rhymes are not only an important part of our oral traditions of the past, but also present ways of memorising and assisting recall, which are invaluable tools in mental mathematics.

Activity *The sandwich game*

LEARNING OBJECTIVES

Understand the vocabulary of comparing and ordering numbers
Compare two familiar numbers, say which is more or less, and give a number which lies between them

Resources

- *Two triangles of foam sheeting to make two bread triangles for a sandwich; card pieces with numerals 0 to 20 on them*

- Show the children the 'bread' for the 'sandwich'. Assign each bread piece a card number (with only one number in between them, for example, 11 and 13). Ask the children what makes the 'filling' in the sandwich. Select the appropriate number (12) and place it between the 'bread slices'. Do this a number of times.

Watch Points

The props can eventually be abandoned and, over many sessions, the children can play 'the sandwich game'. You can simply call out two numbers, and the class or individuals call out what number comes in between.

Activity *Number targets*

LEARNING OBJECTIVES

Understand the vocabulary of comparing and ordering numbers
Compare two familiar numbers, say which is more or less, and give a number which lies between them
Order numbers to at least 20

Resources

- *Blackboard or large blank number track*

- Call out a number. Then ask a child to call out one number that is more and one that is less than your number. Thus if the number called is 20, a child might say:

  20 is more than 2 and less than 24.

  The next child is then not allowed to use 2 or 24 in their answer. As the children take their turns, the numbers they use can be written up, in order, on the blackboard or large blank number track.

- Discuss with the children where each number should be placed on the blackboard, thereby checking children's knowledge of the order of numbers to at least 20.

Watch Points

In subsequent sessions you could repeat the activity asking children to name numbers which come in between two others.

Activity *Written numbers*

LEARNING OBJECTIVE

Read and write numbers to at least 100 *in figures and words*

- Play 'Number Match'. Attach Blu-Tack© to the 0 to 9 and 1 to 9 cards and to one set of the one to nine and twenty to ninety cards. Assemble a batch of matching numeral and word cards for two-digit numbers. For example, cards with 2 and 4 on them could be set out as 24 or 42. Make sure there are corresponding numbers in the word set, such as twenty and four or forty and two.

- Put the cards where the children can see them. Ask one child to move the numbers around to make a numeral and word match. Thus '24' could be set alongside 'twenty-four'. The rest of the class can call out the numbers and evaluate the work of the child at the front.

- In another session play 'Word Match'. Use only the word cards (one to nine and twenty to ninety). Give half the class one to nine cards and the other half twenty to ninety cards. The children should find a partner to make a number more than twenty. Then they can hold up their cards in turn, and call out the number they have made.

Resources

- *Blu-Tack©; sets of number cards: 0 to 9 and 1 to 9; sets of word cards: one to nine and twenty to ninety. Make these cards, or use STPM Year 1* ***Resources****. Make a card for each child in the class. Two sets of each will yield 34 cards (18 and 16). For a class of more than 32 children you need three sets of the twenty to ninety cards. For more than 36 you need three sets of the 1 to 9 cards.*

Watch Points

To reinforce children's written recording, ask individual children at the end of 'Word Match' to write the digits for their number names on the board.

Activity *Tens and ones*

LEARNING OBJECTIVES

Know what each digit in a two-digit number represents, including 0 as a place holder, *and partition two-digit numbers into a multiple of ten and ones (TU)*
Say the number that is 1 or 10 more or less than any given two-digit number

Resources

- *Number cards from 11 to 99*

Watch Points

The game can be repeated if children are given different cards. Because this game involves a great deal of questioning, allow the children some thinking time between each challenge. This will enable you to identify those children who may need particular support in subsequent lessons.

- Shuffle the cards and give the children one each. Call out challenges. If the challenge applies, children should hold up their card for you to see. Here are some example challenges:

  Who has two tens in their number?

  Who has fewer than six tens in their number?

  Who has more than three tens?

  Has your number got no units?

  Has your number got the same number of ones as tens?

  If you added one to your number...

  Who would have five tens?

  Who would then have two ones?

  Whose number would then have the same number of ones as tens?

  Whose number would then 'go up' a ten?

  If you added ten to your number...

  Who would have more than five tens?

  Whose number would then have the same number of ones as tens?

  Has anyone been unable to show his or her card? What is the number?

  Support: display class number lines initially to allow children to look at the sequence or numbers.

Activity *Number line*

LEARNING OBJECTIVE

***Order whole numbers to at least 100**, and position them on a number line and 100 square*

- First, use the numbered side of the line. In turn, give the children a number card. Ask them to clip it to the correct place on the line. For example:

- After several sessions like this, turn the line over. Ask the children to remember their card and then clip it to the line at the point where they judge their particular number should go. For example:

How accurate are the children's estimates?

Support: a 0–20 number line might be used to order the numbers from 0–20.

Resources

- *Number cards from 1 to 99; clothes pegs, paper or bulldog clips for children to attach cards to the line; card number line to stretch across the classroom. It can be laid on the floor or attached to string looped over strong cup hooks in a taut line. Mark one side of the number line from zero to 100 in equal divisions (not all the numbers need to be written in). Mark the other side with divisions, but only write zero and 100 on it.*

Watch Points

Numbers on the number line must be attached to points on the line and not spaces. The card should extend beyond zero and 100, to show that the line continues in both directions.

Activity *Estimating length*

LEARNING OBJECTIVES

Understand and use the vocabulary of estimation
Give a sensible estimate of a number of objects that can be checked by counting
Measure using uniform non-standard units

Resources

- *A copy of the 'Counting steps' rhyme*

- Teach the children the 'Counting steps' rhyme:

  How many steps do I have to take
  To get from here to the door?
  Please count how many steps I take
  Walking across the floor.
  1, 2, 3, . . .

- Ask a child to stand some distance from the classroom door. Ask for estimates of how many steps it will take him or her to reach the door. Then ask the children to sing the song and count along as the child steps to the door. Vary the starting points for other children.

- Rhymes to fit other distances and lengths around the school can be created with the class. For example:

  How many thumbs (or cubits or feet or paces)
  Do you think might
  Fit the book (or bench or carpet or doorway)
  And measure right?

- In each case an individual child can estimate the measure identified by the rhyme. Then another child can do the measuring while the rest of the class look on and count.

Watch Points

The *Framework for Teaching Mathematics* includes many ideas for appropriate non-standard units of length. You should also offer some uniform non-standard units to estimate and measure, for example, straws, rulers, garden canes.

Emphasise the use of appropriate vocabulary throughout the activity (for example, 'nearly', 'roughly', 'close to').

ESTIMATING AND ROUNDING

Activity *Estimating measures*

LEARNING OBJECTIVES

Understand and use the vocabulary of estimation
Give a sensible estimate of a number of objects that can be checked by counting

- Divide the children into groups. Hold up a 'bundle' of items, such as pencils, in one hand. Ask them to agree an estimate of the number of items in their groups. Each group says what their estimate is and then the items are counted to see which group was nearest.
- Play the game several times, collecting a bundle of a different size each time.

Resources

- *Pencils, paintbrushes or rulers (or other classroom items that can be held in one hand as a 'bunch'). There should be about 30 items of one kind.*

Watch Points

In other sessions, the groups could estimate how many are left when some are taken away from the bundle.

Activity *Making estimates*

LEARNING OBJECTIVE

Give a sensible estimate of at least 50 objects

- Hold up a card with a small number of stickers on it. Give the children a few seconds to look at it. Cover the card and ask individuals to estimate how many stickers they saw. Continue to ask children until there are no more different estimates. Write the estimates up on the board. Ask the class for a show of hands for each estimate given.
- Discuss how children arrived at their estimates. Talk about the methods used, and point out that they can make comparisons with counts they know, and think about how the number of objects fit a space.
- Hold up the card and count the stickers with the children. Display the card after the lesson, so individuals can check the count for themselves.
- Choose another card and repeat the activity.

Resources

- *Sheets of stickers with a wide variety of images. Stick different numbers of stickers on to cards in rows, columns and irregular groups. Make as many as possible, including some with up to 50 stickers.*

Watch Points

The children may note that the arrangement of the stickers in rows or columns makes estimating easier.

As an alternative to recording the estimates on a board, you could use a number line.

Activity *Rounding up and down*

LEARNING OBJECTIVES

Use and begin to read the vocabulary of estimation and approximation
Round numbers less than 100 to the nearest 10

- Choose one batch of cards (for example, the 20 to 30 batch). Remove the tens cards from that batch and give them to two children who should stand in front of the class. Then hand out the other cards, one at a time, asking what the number is and questions such as:

  Are we going to round up or down?

  Is this number nearer to 20 or nearer to 30?

  Where should it go? With the 20 or the 30?

- When the children say to which tens number their card is nearest, they can give it to the person holding the appropriate tens card. For example, if Melinda holds the 20 card and Jerry the 30 card at the front, children should give cards 21, 22, 23, and 24 to Melinda and 25, 26, 27, 28 and 29 to Jerry.

- Begin the game again with another batch of cards.

Resources

- *Cards with two-digit numbers on them. Include all the counting numbers from 10 to 100. Make the multiples of 10 cards in a different colour and make two sets each of the tens cards from 20 to 90. Store them in batches of 11 thus: 10 to 20, 20 to 30, 30 to 40, 40 to 50, 50 to 60, 60 to 70, 70 to 80, 80 to 90, 90 to 100.*

Watch Points

Make sure children are familiar with approximation, rounding up and rounding before starting this game. At the end of Year 2, some children may still require support in this area.

Activity *Half and quarter*

LEARNING OBJECTIVES

Begin to recognise and find one half and one quarter of shapes and small numbers of objects
Begin to recognise that two halves or four quarters make one whole and that two quarters and one half are equivalent

- Lay out some or all of the resources (omitting the 'quarters') on a table at the front of the class. Take up one whole item and show the children. If it is the length of string, ribbon or wool, ask the children to picture in their heads what half the length would look like, and then to hold out both hands to show the length they were thinking of. Then ask a child to come to the front and find the card with half the length on it.

- If the item is a clock or a card shape, again ask the children to picture in their mind's eye what half of it looks like. They can then all try to trace the shape in the air using a pointing or 'magic finger'. Again ask a child to select and hold up the half that goes with the whole.

- This activity can be conducted over several sessions. A variation involves holding up a half and asking the children to visualise what the whole will look like.

Resources

- *Create and laminate the following cards: one card with a length of string, two cards with half that length, four cards with a quarter of that length; similar sets of whole-, half- and quarter- length cards for differing lengths of ribbon and wool; a clock face, two half faces (cut through the twelve) and four quarter faces cut through twelve, three, six and nine. Cut and laminate a square, a rectangle, a circle, a triangle and two halves and four quarters of each of these shapes.*

Watch Points

When the children are competent with wholes and halves, try working with wholes and quarters, and then have sessions working with wholes, halves and quarters.

These exercises will also help to assess children's knowledge of fractions in 'real life' contexts.

Activity *Number fractions*

LEARNING OBJECTIVE

Begin to recognise and find one half and one quarter of small numbers of objects

- Remove from the stack an even number of yoghurt pots and set them out on the table. Ask a child to count the pots by counting in ones, or counting in her or his head. Then the child should pile the pots into two sets of equal size and say the number of each half set. The discussion may go as follows:

  Sadiya, please come and set out and count these pots.
  How many are there in total? (16)
  Show us half of these 16 pots. How many are there? (Eight)
  Now Sadiya, show us half of eight pots. How many is that? (Four)
  And what is half of four? And half of two?

- This same activity can then be repeated using any even number up to 30.

Resources

- *Thirty empty yoghurt pots (clean the outside, or cover with paper). Those shaped like truncated cones are good as they stack easily.*

Watch Points

You can repeat the activity asking the children to display and demonstrate quarters using the same pots. Are the children able to write the results of the activity on the board using the correct notation for $\frac{1}{2}$ and $\frac{1}{4}$?

Activity *One more*

LEARNING OBJECTIVES

Begin to use the vocabulary involved in adding
Find one more or one less than a number
Begin to relate addition to counting on

- Begin by calling out numbers to the class and asking the children to say the number that is one more than the number called.

  For example, 4:

  5 is *one more* than 4.

  Then allow a child a turn at calling the numbers.

- Give every child a number card at random and ask them to pair up so that one of the pair of numbers is one more than the other. Ask the children to hold up their numbers and go around the class asking all the children to read them out in turn.

  Support: instead of number cards give the children picture cards. They will then be able to count the number of objects on the card.

Resources

- *Number cards. They can be numbers in sequence from one to the total number of children in the class, a sequence starting with a number other than one (for example, 21), or numbers at random. If you choose the latter option, half the cards should carry numbers and the other half those numbers plus and minus 1. Thus, if 29 is on a card 28 or 30 should also be chosen.*

Watch Points

There may be a problem at the beginning or end of a sequence; for example, if '2' gets together with '3', and so on a child with a card marked '1' will be left out. If this happens simply point out what has happened and why.

Activity *Take one*

LEARNING OBJECTIVES

Begin to use the vocabulary involved in subtracting
Find one less than a number from 1 to 10
Begin to relate subtraction to 'taking away'

Resources

- *Ten cakes, jam tarts or buns made from play dough*

- Lay the buns out on the front table. Ask the children how many there are, and then allow ten children to take one each in turn, while the other children call out what is left.

- As the game goes along, stop the action and ask questions using important vocabulary such as:

  There are six buns. Jo *ate one* bun. How many buns *are left*?

  What is four buns *take away one* bun?

  What is *one less* than two buns?

  How many buns *are gone*?

Extension: repeat the exercise, extending the vocabulary involved (for example, 'subtract', 'minus').

Watch Points

Lay the buns out again. Let one child do the actions and announce, 'Ten buns take away one bun is nine' and so on.

Encourage the whole class to count the new totals:

'We ate four of our ten buns. How many buns are left? Count: 1, 2, 3, 4, 5, 6.'

Activity *Adding two groups*

LEARNING OBJECTIVES

Begin to use the vocabulary involved in adding
Begin to relate addition to combining two groups of objects, counting all the objects

Resources

- *A group of up to 10 objects – coloured balls, small soft toys, pencils*

- Put the children into two groups and hand out objects randomly. Ask some children in a group to place their objects in a set, and some from the other group to do likewise. Then ask the whole class to calculate the total.

- Question the children as the calculations are done, so that they hear the ways we use mathematical vocabulary, such as:

  How many are in the red group's set? (3 pencils)

  How many have the green group put out? (6 pencils)

  What is the sum of 6 and 3?

  What is the total?

  What is 6 plus 3?

  How many pencils altogether?

Extension: repeat the activity using a greater number of objects, so that the total is, for example, 15. Repeat the activity using three groups of objects.

Watch Points

Encourage all the children to count the totals, and then to repeat them using whole sentences. For example:
'Count: 1, 2, 3, 4, 5.
Say altogether: 3 add 2 is 5.'

Activity *Practical subtraction*

LEARNING OBJECTIVES

Begin to use the vocabulary involved in subtracting
Remove a smaller number from a larger and find how many are left by counting back from the larger number

Resources

- *Ten apples or oranges*

- Place the fruit on the table so that all the children can see it. Invite one child to take away one piece of fruit at a time, while the children call out what is left.

- Use questions as the calculations are done, such as:

  How many apples are on the table?

  Take one away. How many are left?

  How many did we begin with?

  How many has Gemma taken away?

  If Sam puts them all back, how many will there be?

Activity *Adding using a number track*

LEARNING OBJECTIVE

Understand the operation of addition *(counting on steps along a number line)*

Resources

- *A number track as shown in 'One to twenty' (page 13)*

- Point to a number on the track. Ask the children what the total will be if another number is added to the first number. Indicate by jumping a finger along the track so that the addition can be shown. For example:

  If we begin with six, (point to six) **and add three, what is the total?** (Nine)

  Nine, that's right. We can show this by starting at six, and making three jumps; six, seven (one jump), **eight** (two jumps), **nine** (three jumps). **So six add three is nine.**

- Invite individual children to show how other additions can be done using this method.

Watch Points

Include some additions involving zero.

When the children understand the concept, show them how to count back on a number line in order to 'take away'.

Activity *Domino difference*

LEARNING OBJECTIVES

Understand the operation of addition *(combining two sets to make a total)* ***and use the related vocabulary***
Understand the operation of subtraction (as 'difference') and use the related vocabulary

Resources

- *Dominoes – one per child. (There are 28 in a set, so include more than one set if necessary.)*

Watch Points

In other sessions, repeat the activity, this time asking the children to find the difference between the number of dots on the halves of their dominoes.

- Ask the children to sit in a circle and give them each a domino, which they may look at, but should not let the other children see. Begin by asking the children in turn to describe their domino. Without revealing the face of the domino, they should say in turn, how many dots there are on each half of the domino, and how many there are in total. They then hold up the domino to show the class.

- When several children have done this, ask the next child to say what is on one half of the domino, and then relate the total number of dots. The class can then call out what they think is on the remaining half.

- When several children have done this, ask all the children questions so that they can show their domino.

  For example:

  Who has a three?
  Who has a zero?
  Who has a number more than two?
  Hold up your domino if the dots on it total six.

Activity: *Number pairs to ten*

LEARNING OBJECTIVES

Know by heart addition facts for all pairs with a total of 10 (for example, 3 + 7)
Begin to know addition and subtraction facts for all pairs of numbers with a total up to at least 10

Resources

- *A copy of 'Here comes the bus' and 'Crocodile' (see **Count Me In: 44 Songs and Rhymes about Numbers**)*

- Using the rhymes, work with the children on the pairs of numbers making all totals up to ten, by changing the numbers in the rhymes each time.
- **Here comes the bus**

  Here comes the bus
  It's going to stop.
  Hurry up children,
  In you pop.
  Four inside
  And six on top.
  How many altogether?
- **Crocodile**

  A happy green crocodile
  Eats three men.
  Then he has the others – how many
  To make up to ten?

Watch Points

The children could help to make up some of their own class rhymes using the ideas shown here.

Activity: *Snakes and adders*

LEARNING OBJECTIVES

Understand the operation of addition and use the related vocabulary
Begin to recognise that addition can be done in any order

Resources

- *A card snake, about 50 cm long, with an open mouth*

- Write two numbers on the board. Explain that the snake is an 'adder' so he adds up numbers. But he always swallows the bigger number first. Ask which is the bigger of the two numbers. Make the snake gobble that number and then ask a child to do the addition. Discuss how they did it.
- Ask another child to do the addition by taking the smaller number first. Ask whether the answer should be the same. Discuss which order of taking the numbers is easier.
- Give the snake to a child. Write another pair of numbers on the board, and allow the child holding the adder to lead the 'adder addition'.

Watch Points

Reinforce that there are a variety of possible methods for adding two numbers and that children should find the ways they find easiest but it is often easier to work from the bigger number first.

Activity *Dice totals*

LEARNING OBJECTIVES

Extend understanding of the operation of addition
Begin to add three single-digit numbers mentally (totals up to 20)

- Using one of the sets of equipment ask two children to help throw the dice and spin the spinner repeatedly. The numbers that come up should be added together. The whole class may call out the answers or hold up their number cards at first. Then challenges may be addressed to individual children.

  Extension: repeat the activity this time rolling the dice three times, making three numbers for the children to add together.

Resources

- *For different sessions prepare the following: an octahedral floor dice with the numbers 1 to 8 on it and a floor spinner marked 0, 1, 2, 0, 1, 2 (a floor spinner can be made using a large regular hexagon and a pencil or pea stick.); a cube floor dice marked 1 to 6 and a floor spinner marked 0, 1, 2, 3, 4, 0; two floor dice marked 0 to 5; number cards 1–20 (optional)*

Watch Points

If we look just at number pairs, there are 54 possible additions to make numbers up to ten. The resources for this lesson should give children the chance to try all these additions.

Blank dice are useful for this type of game, as they allow you to choose the numbers.

Activity *Tri-dice*

LEARNING OBJECTIVES

Extend understanding of the operation of addition
Understand that more than two numbers can be added
Begin to add three single-digit numbers mentally (totals up to about 20) or three two-digit numbers with the help of apparatus (totals up to 100)
Use knowledge that addition can be done in any order: *put the largest first and/or find a pair totalling ten*

- Throw all three dice, or ask a child to do so, and ask the children to sum the totals that arise.

- Do this repeatedly over many sessions and see how many the children can complete in, for example, five minutes.

Resources

- *Two dice (small or floor dice) and a blank dice marked in dots or numerals to show 0, 1, 2, 7, 8 and 9*

Watch Points

This type of exercise offers a useful formative assessment opportunity and can be used over a number of lessons to check children's rapid recall of addition facts. QCA's *Teaching mental strategies* describes what calculation facts children are expected to recall rapidly on a year-by-year basis.

Activity *Just checking*

LEARNING OBJECTIVE

Repeat addition in a different order (checking results)

- Divide the class into four groups. Give each group a pile of calculation cards, which they place face down on a table. Ask one group to pick up a card and call out the answer. Then choose another group and repeat the calculation with the numbers in a different order so that the answers given by the first group can be checked.
- For example, if the card reads 11 + 6, the first group should say 17. Say to another group:

  Try 6 + 11. What is your answer?

  Is it the same as the first group's answer?

  Can you tell me how you did it?

Resources

- *Cards with calculations on them (but no answers). In the example shown here, some of the number bonds to ten are used.*

Watch Points

The calculations can be chosen to match the work the children have been doing, both in terms of the numbers and the way they are set out.

Activity *Check it out!*

LEARNING OBJECTIVES

Repeat addition or multiplication in a different order
Check with an equivalent calculation (checking results)

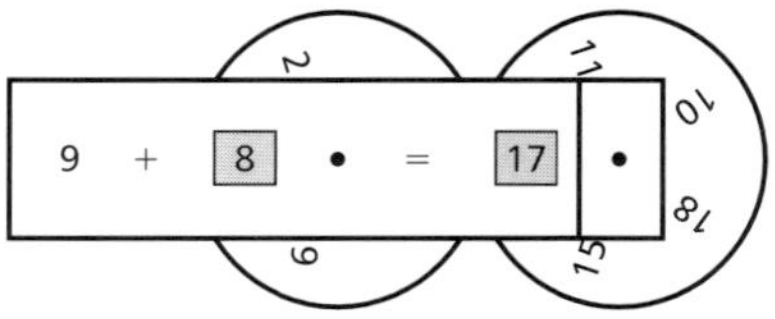

- Hold up a calculation card, or ask a child to hold it up, and cover the answer. Ask an individual to solve it. Ask how they worked it out. Ask another child to check the calculation. Let them talk about their methods of checking the answer. Ask for other suggestions of ways to check an answer.

  Repeat this game with another card, or if using a card like the one above, vary the figures, sometimes producing a calculation with a wrong answer, which the first child asked needs to correct.

Resources

- *Large cards with calculations on them. These can be made as shown.*

Watch Points

The initial questions might be set as a number story, for example 'There were 21 people on a bus. 9 people got off. How many are on the bus now?'
21 − 9 = 12
Check with 21 − 10 + 1.

Activity *Larger first*

LEARNING OBJECTIVE

Use knowledge that addition can be done in any order to do mental calculations more efficiently. For example: put the larger number first and count on in ones, including beyond 10

Resources

- *Number cards (1–10) and addition sign cards. Make these, or use STPM Reception, Year 1 or Year 2* ***Resources****.*

- Shuffle the cards and place them face down on the table at the front of the class. Invite two children to take the top two cards and show them to the class. They should then stand side by side.
- Point out that if we want to add these numbers, it might be helpful to put the bigger number first. Ask which that is. Ask the child with the bigger number to stand on the left (from the children's point of view). Then hold the addition sign in the gap between the children and invite the children to count on aloud until they have a total. Thus, if Mark has a 5 card and Lisa draws a 9 card, Lisa should stand on the left and Mark on the right and the children should count 9, 10, 11, 12, 13, 14.
- After several goes the children should be able to examine their numbers and place themselves in order so that the class can count on.

Extension: repeat the activity using numbers up to 20 and/or three single-digit numbers.

Activity *Function machines*

LEARNING OBJECTIVE

Find the difference between a positive and a negative integer

Resources

- *A large cardboard box, Multilink©, Unifix© or other similar apparatus, small cards with addition or subtraction 'functions' on them, such as +2, −3*

- Put the box where children can see it. Stick a 'function' card (for example '+1') on the front of the box. Explain that this is an 'Add one' box. What goes into the box has one added to it before it comes out. Show the children one Multilink©. Place it in the box and pull out two, put in two and pull out three, put in three and pull out four. Ask the children to predict how the pattern of calculations continues.
- Then change the function card, and begin another pattern.

Watch Points

The STPM *Year 2 Number* textbook includes some more of these function machine problems.

Activity *Partitioning*

LEARNING OBJECTIVE

Use knowledge that addition can be done in any order to do mental calculations more efficiently. For example: begin to partition into 5 and a bit when adding 6, 7, 8 or 9, then recombine

- With the children's help create a chart on the board as follows:

  6 = 5 + 1
  7 = 5 + 2
  8 = 5 + 3
  9 = 5 + 4

- Then in quick succession call out some of the following calculations for everyone to try to answer:

6 + 7	6 + 8	6 + 9
7 + 6	8 + 6	9 + 6
7 + 8	7 + 9	8 + 9
8 + 7	9 + 7	9 + 8

- Ask individual children for their answers and write them on the board. Ask them to explain how they worked them out. Point out that these numbers can be 'broken' into '5 + a bit' to make the addition easier.

  Support: if the children find these tasks too hard, create some problems where the children will only need to partition one of the numbers at first (for example, 5 + 6, 5 + 7).

Watch Points

Individual children may offer other equally valid methods of working out these addition facts. Ask them to explain their alternative strategies. Point out that nine is only one less than ten and that when adding nine, it may prove easier to add ten and then subtract one before giving the answer.

Activity *Nearly tens*

LEARNING OBJECTIVE

Add 9 to single-digit numbers by adding 10 then subtracting 1

- Adding 1, 2 or 3 to 9 is quick to do by counting on. The children can practise adding 4, 5, 6, 7 and 8 to 9 by other means. Here are some possible methods:

  – Add the number to 10 and then subtract 1.
  – In adding 5 to 9 use the counting pattern of 5s or 5 + 10 to reach 15 and subtract 1.
  – In adding 6 to 9 use 5 + 1 + 5 + 4 to make 10 + 5.
  – In adding 8 to 9 they will see that this is nearly 9 + 9 then subtract 1.

- Do some of the following calculations, writing them one at a time on the board:

4 + 9	5 + 9	6 + 9	7 + 9	8 + 9
9 + 4	9 + 5	9 + 6	9 + 7	9 + 8

  Ask the children to think of as many ways as they can of doing each one, and to explain these mental strategies.

  Extension: the exercise can be repeated by adding 9 to two-digit numbers, for example, 35 + 9 = 35 + 10 − 1.

Watch Points

Adding 9 by adding 10 then subtracting 1 is also known as 'compensation'. Discuss the calculations so that the children can suggest their own strategies. Ask the children which they think is easiest and why.

Activity *Take away patterns*

LEARNING OBJECTIVE

Use patterns of similar calculations (for example, 10 − 0 = 10, 10 − 1 = 9, 10 − 2 = 8)

- Divide the class in half down the middle of the room, and ask the children in both halves to sit facing one another. Ask one half of the class to call out a pattern of 'take-aways'. For example:

  Nine take away zero is ...
  Nine take away one is ...
  Nine take away two is ... (continuing until)
  Nine take away nine is ...

  For each calculation the other half of the class should call out the answer at the appropriate moment.

- The game can be played with new starting numbers and the halves of the class can swop roles.
- Other patterns can also be recited in this way, for example:

  Nine take away one is ...
  Eight take away one is ...
  Seven take away one is ...

  Twelve take away three is ...
  Nine take away three is ...
  Six take away three is ...

- The game can be played in other ways. For example:
  - One half of the class completes a calculation, and the other half does the next
  - Boys give the calculation and girls answer (and vice versa)
  - Each child in one half of the class starts a number sentence, which is completed by a child in the other half of the room.

Watch Points

Addition patterns can be worked on in the same way. An adult could write the number facts on the board as the children offer them.

Activity *Number tree*

LEARNING OBJECTIVE

Use known number facts and place value to add or subtract a pair of numbers mentally within the range zero to at least 10, then zero to at least 20

- Hang the card with 2 on it on the tree. Tell the children that you wish to 'make five'. Invite them to suggest what other number(s) might be hung on the tree to make this total. Try out all the suggestions the children make. Discuss with the children any remaining ways of making five.
- Alter the target total to six and begin the game again.

Extension: later you can include additional cards with numbers from 10 to 20 in the box. You could set a target total for the 'Number tree' every day.

Resources

- *A card tree outline, with paper fasteners attached. Number cards, each with a string loop so they can be 'hung' on the tree. For first sessions the numerals should include several sets of the numerals from zero to ten. Make these cards or use STPM Year 1* ***Resources****.*

Watch Points

In a series of sessions, and sometimes using children to place the numbers on the tree, all combinations of numbers to 10 and then to 20 can be tried.

Activity *Bridging ten*

LEARNING OBJECTIVE

Begin to bridge through 10, and later 20, when adding a single-digit number

- Invite the children to sit in a circle. Write a starter number between 6 and 9, on the board. Throw the dice into the circle and ask the children to add the number showing uppermost on the dice to the starter number. Then ask a child to throw the dice for the next calculation.
- After several goes change the starter number.
- Ask individual children how they tackled each one, and try to establish one method as the following:

  For 6 + 8, I can make 10 by adding 2 to 8, and then I need to add 4 more.

Extension: when the children are all quick and confident at bridging 10, try bridging through 20 using the same game.

Resources

- *A blank floor dice marked with 4, 5, 6, 7, 8, 9*

Watch Points

Some children will still be counting on in ones at this stage. These children may require some additional support in subsequent lessons.

You might prompt the children as follows 'You know that 6 + 4 = 10, so what is 6 + 8?'

Activity *Make 20*

LEARNING OBJECTIVES

Know by heart all pairs of numbers with a total of 20 (for example, 13 + 7)
Know by heart all pairs of multiples of 10 with a total of 100 (for example, 30 + 70)

Watch Points

In another session ask the children to tackle number pairs using multiples of ten to 100.

- Ask the children to sit in a circle. Select a child to start the activity and give them a number between 1 and 20. The child should use that number to make a number sentence with a total of 20. For example:

  Barbara, your start number is eleven.
  Eleven and nine make twenty/Eleven plus nine make twenty.

  The child next to Barbara then takes eleven plus one as a start number, thus:

  Twelve and eight make twenty.

  Continue the game until it reaches:

  Twenty and zero make twenty.

  The next child takes twenty minus one as the start number, so:

  Nineteen and one make twenty.

  Continue the game around the circle several times.

Activity *What's the difference?*

LEARNING OBJECTIVE

Find a small difference by counting up from the smaller to the larger number

Watch Points

Highlight the fact that the children have been able to find the answer to a subtraction question by counting on. Write the number fact on the board: 42 − 37 = 5. This strategy is very effective when two numbers are close together, for example, 53 − 49.

- Ask the children to sit in a circle. Set a challenge to find the difference between two numbers (making the difference between five and ten). One child begins by repeating the challenge. The counting on then begins with each child putting up his or her hand as they call out his or her number. When the target number is reached, the next child counts up the raised hands to find the difference. Another challenge can be issued and the game restarted. Here is an example game:

- Teacher: **What is the difference between 42 and 37? Megan, can you start?**
  Megan: **The difference between 42 and 37. Count on from 37.**
  Jo: **38** (puts hand up)
  Liam: **39** (puts hand up)
  Ishmail: **40** (puts hand up)
  Sukim: **41** (puts hand up)
  Eve: **42** (puts hand up)
  Fiona: (counts out loud the raised hands) **The difference between 37 and 42 is 5.**

MENTAL STRATEGIES (+ AND –)

Activity *Bits and pieces*

LEARNING OBJECTIVE

Use a range of mental strategies for addition and subtraction

- Give children the opportunity to do a range of different calculations. Fix the card stars around the room – you could fix enough for a whole week of short oral sessions (say 20 calculations) in one go. Here is a set of examples:

  Add 6, 7, 8 or 9

16 + 6	22 + 7	7 + 13
8 + 23	44 +8	9 + 27

  Partition numbers into tens and units

32 + 17	57 – 33	23 + 65
83 – 52	44 – 22	62 + 36

  Add or subtract 9 or 19, 11 or 21

9 + 42	19 + 16	21 – 7
11 + 21	9 + 53	11 – 4

- At the start of each session, point to a calculation and ask the children to do it in their heads. Ask an individual child for the answer, and to say how they worked it out. Ask the rest of the class if anyone used a different method. Ask the child to describe his or her method.
- Over many sessions, allow the children to try several calculations each session, and share methods they find easiest.

Resources

- *Write out some addition and subtraction number sentences on card stars. These should include examples where the children have the opportunity to add 6, 7, 8 or 9, partition numbers into tens and units, and add or subtract 9, 19, 11 or 21.*

Watch Points

In discussions, encourage the children to partition their additions or use compensation strategies. Focus in particular on any of the cards the children found difficult and find out why.

For reinforcement, in some of these sessions you might ask the children to think of a 'number story' to go with the addition/subtraction fact. For example, 'I had 21 computer games, but I sold 9 to my friend. I have 12 computer games left.'

Activity *Lots of*

LEARNING OBJECTIVES

Understand the operation of multiplication as repeated addition

Use and begin to read the related vocabulary

Resources

- *Sets of classroom objects, for example, pens, books or rulers*

- Invite one child to stand in front of the others. Tell the children they are to look carefully and answer some questions:

  How many *eyes* has Jamil got?

  How many *ears* has Jamil got?

  How many *arms* has Jamil got?

  How many *hands* has Jamil got?

  How many *legs* has Jamil got?

  How many *feet* has Jamil got?

- Point out that Jamil has one set of eyes, or 'one *lot of* two eyes'. Make similar statements for the other features the children have counted.

- Then invite another child to join Jamil. Now ask the children, for example, how many eyes, ears, there are altogether. Jamil has one 'lot' of two eyes, Laura has one 'lot' of two eyes. Thus we can say:

  Two lots of two make four.

  2 times 2 is the same as $2 + 2$

- Ask individual children to complete statements about the other features counted. Continue to add children to the row until there are five children:

  Five lots of two eyes.

  5 times 2 is the same as $2 + 2 + 2 + 2 + 2$

- Find some objects to be grouped in threes. Begin as above with three, and add a group of three at a time so that the children can see the groups of three build up.

Watch Points

This same game can also be repeated for fours.

Use children's hands to work up to 'ten lots of five fingers'. You might record the children's oral responses on the board, perhaps drawing the hands with 'one lot of five fingers' below each hand.

Activity Sharing

LEARNING OBJECTIVES

Understand the operation of division as sharing
Use and begin to read the related vocabulary

- Tell the children to look carefully at the whole pizza picture and think about what the pieces would look like if the pizza was shared between two children. Allow them to use their pointing fingers to draw the pizza shapes in the air. Ask a child to draw the shape on the board. Check that the rest of the class agree. Show the children the two half pieces placed together and then show one piece as a 'share'. Ask how much of the whole pizza this is. Then show the children one of the quarter pictures and say:

  If some children shared the pizza and they all had a piece like this, how many children were sharing?

- In another session ask two, three, four or six children to stand in front of the class. Hand out the sweets to these children while asking questions such as:

  How many children are sharing?
  How many sweets have I got?
  How many shares are there?
  How many sweets will Megan have?
  Will there be any sweets left over if they are shared equally?
  Have all the children got the same number of sweets?

Resources

- *A bag of twelve sweets or cakes made from salt and flour dough; a card pizza, a similar picture cut into two halves and a third picture cut into four quarters (you could use the lids of supermarket pizzas.)*

Watch Points

It may also be useful to model the answer on the blackboard with the children's help. For example: '4 sweets are shared between 2 children. How many does each child get?'

Activity Sharing and grouping

LEARNING OBJECTIVE

Understand the operation of division as sharing equally

- Use Blu-Tack© to mount your plate on the board to use as a demonstration. Show the children that they are going to be sharing out some different food items. Ask them to work in pairs to set out the food helpings. Here is an example.

  Set out in front of you both four eggs, eight fairy cakes and six samosas.

  Now share out the eggs equally. How many each? (two).

  So four eggs shared between two is two each. In maths we call this division.

  Now share out the fairy cakes and samosas equally between two children. How many does each child get?

  Extension: this game can be repeated for a range of small shares between two. In subsequent sessions, the children can get into threes, fours or fives and look at how, for example, eight chocolate bars are shared equally between four children.

Resources

- *Paper plates, one for you and one for each child; food pictures (mounted on card and laminated), such as: apples, eggs, chocolate bars, packets of crisps, bananas, yoghurts (you need two sets of these for every child)*

Watch Points

This activity could also introduce children to the idea of 'grouping' or 'repeated subtraction'. For example, 'If there are ten sweets in a jar, how many bags of five sweets can I make?'

Activity *Bullfrogs and tadpoles*

LEARNING OBJECTIVE

Know by heart doubles of all numbers to 10 and the corresponding halves

- Lay out the Set 1 'bullfrog' cards face up around the room at random. Select one child to be a bullfrog and ask her to collect all her numbered cards (or 'gold pieces'). However, in 'bullfrog world' everything appears twice as big as it really is. So, every time she picks up a gold piece she must show it to the class and tell them what that number is in 'bullfrog world' (that is, double it) before she can take it. As the 'bullfrog' child can see all of the numbers on the gold pieces, she can be asked to collect them in order.

- In subsequent sessions give out the Set 2 'tadpole' cards to individual children, and then distribute the matching 'bullfrog' (2–20) cards to the remaining children. Invite each 'tadpole' to find his or her 'bullfrog' (that is, the person holding the card that has the double of his or her number on it). In the meantime, of course, the bullfrogs are also searching for their tadpoles – the child holding the card with a number on it that is half of their own. Children without a card can watch the action and go around checking the number cards when all the children have paired up.

  Support: to focus on addition doubles to 5 + 5, limit the two initial sets of cards to 5 and the third 'bullfrog' set to 10.

Resources

- *Two differently coloured sets of number cards (1–10). Set 1 will be the bullfrogs, and Set 2 will be the tadpoles. Make a third set of number cards (2, 4, 6, 8, 10, 12, 14, 16, 18, 20).*

Watch Points

In the first activity the number cards could be placed face down, so that the bullfrog either picks them up at random or has to inspect cards and remember where they are to be able to pick them up in order.

The focus of these activities is on doubling and halving. However, it can also be used to introduce children to 'scaling' which is further explored in Year 3.

Activity *Jumping multiplication*

LEARNING OBJECTIVES

***Understand the operation of multiplication as repeated addition**, and begin to understand division as grouping (repeated subtraction) or sharing*
Use and begin to read the related vocabulary

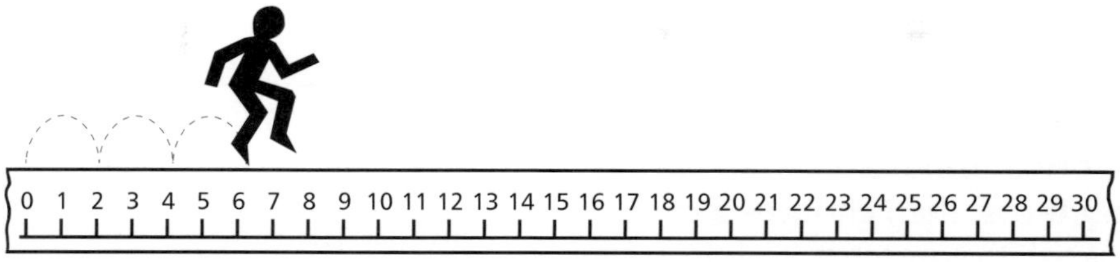

- Call out a multiplication number sentence and jump Jason along the line to show it. Thus, if the multiplication is 3 x 2 he can begin at zero and make three jumps of two to land on six.
- Then start him at zero and add on twos to arrive at the same point on the line.

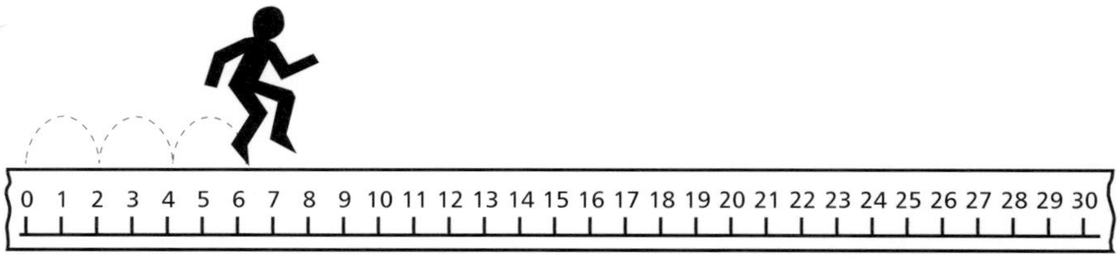

- Do this with several multiplications, and then let the children take turns.

Resources

- *A class number line (0–30), with no divisions between the numbers. Mount the number line on card so children can stand behind it. Make two card figures: Jumping Jason who faces right and will be used for (repeated) addition, and Jumping Julie who faces left and will be used for (repeated) subtraction.*

Watch Points

In a different session try repeated subtraction. Set Julie at, for example, 15, and count down in fives, and then share into fives making the same three jumps.

Activity *Multiple marathon*

LEARNING OBJECTIVES

Know by heart multiplication facts for the 2 and 10 times table

Begin to know multiplication facts for the 5 times table

- The example given here uses the 2 times table. First, ask the children to hold up their two pointing fingers, and bend them up and down as they count in twos up to twenty or beyond.
- Then shuffle the cards and take out two to put aside, face down. One child, or children taking turns, then chooses a card. He or she should say how many 'twos' it represents and prop it up along the blackboard or a shelf, in order.
- When all the cards are set up, a child or the class should say what the numbers on the two missing cards are, and how many 'twos' they represent.
- This game can be repeated, using different players, and with two, four or more cards removed from a set.

Resources

- *Sets of cards each with a product of the following on: 2 times table, 5 times table, 10 times table*

Watch Points

When counting in fives the children can hold up and clench and unclench a fist, revealing five fingers each time a count is made. For tens they can do this action with both hands.

Activity *Show me*

LEARNING OBJECTIVE

Know by heart doubles of all numbers to 10

- Tell the children they will be practising their doubles.
- Start by saying:

  – Show me double one.

  All the children should show the '2' card.
  Place the '2' card in a column underneath the '1' card at the front of the class.

  – Now show me double two.

  All the children should show the '4' card.
  Place the '4' card below the '2'.

  – Show me double four.

  All the children should show the '8' card.
  Place the '8' card below the '4'.

  – Show me double eight.

  All the children should show the '16' card.
  Place the '16' card below the '8'.

- Start another column from double 3 and continue the pattern of doubles until every one from double 1 to double 10 has been chosen.

Extension: if you have laid out the cards in columns, a follow up session might involve individual children responding to targeted questions such as:

Touch 4.

Touch double 4.

Touch half 12.

Resources

- *Number cards 1–20 (one set per child); number cards 1–20 (one enlarged set for the teacher)*

Watch Points

Knowledge of doubles is an essential mathematical skill. Regular practice of the doubles from 1 + 1 to 10 + 10 will help with a range of mental strategies across all four operations. This activity should allow you to make informal assessments of children's recall of doubles to 10 + 10.

The pattern of doubles should be:
Double 1, 2, 4, 8
Double 3, 6, 12
Double 7, 14
Double 9, 18.

Activity *Going in reverse*

LEARNING OBJECTIVES

Know and use halving as the inverse of doubling
Know by heart doubles of all numbers to 10 and the corresponding halves
Use known number facts to carry out mentally multiplications and divisions

Resources

- *Two large flashcards. Flashcard 1 has 'doubled is' on one side and 'halved is' on the other. Flashcard 2 has '×' on one side and '÷' on the other. Blu-Tack© to stick them to the board.*

- Write up a number on the board (for example, 6). Place flashcard 1 ('doubled is') next to it. Ask the children for the answer and write it at the end. For example:

  6 doubled is 12.

  Then write 12 below this. Turn flashcard 1 over ('halved is') and place it alongside. When the children give an answer complete the number sentence like this:

  12 halved is 6.

- Practise with plenty of numbers so the children can see the link between doubles and halves.

- Then try a similar game using multiplication and division. For example write '7' on the board. Place flashcard 2 ('x') next to it and then a '2' number card. When the children answer '14' write up '= 14' to complete the number sentence.

- Then turn flashcard 2 over ('÷'). Ask the children if the numbers in the multiplication number sentence can be moved around to make a division number sentence. The children may help to complete this pattern:

  $7 \times 2 = 14$
  $14 \div 2 = 7$
  $14 \div 7 = 2$

  You can also write up $2 \times 7 = 14$ to make the pattern complete.

- Repeat this game with other example numbers.

Activity *Double trouble*

LEARNING OBJECTIVE

Derive quickly doubles of all numbers to at least 15; doubles of multiples of 5 to 50; halves of multiples of 10 to 100

Resources

- *Make up a large card strip as shown with numbers 1–15 on each side of the closed flaps, and their doubles on the inside.*

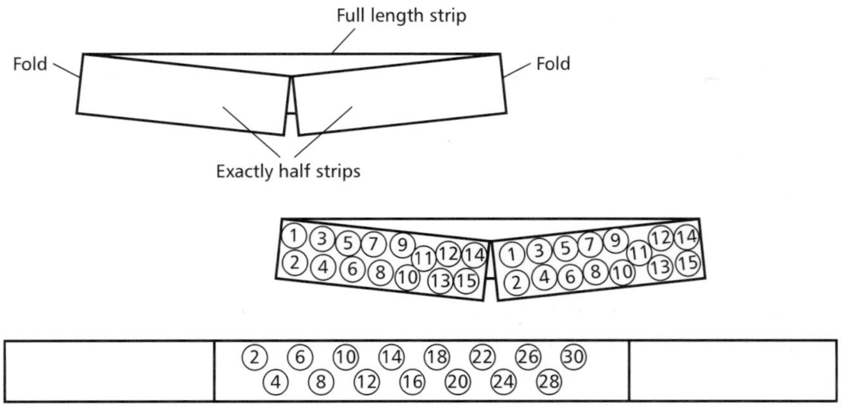

- Point to one of the numbers on the half flap. Ask the children to double it. Open the flaps and find the answer. Repeat this for all numbers to 15 in random order.

- Then try halving by leaving the flaps open. Point to a number and ask:

  What is half ...?

  The answer number will be evident on the fronts of both flaps. Repeat this for all numbers to 15 in random order.

  Extension: in subsequent sessions new flap cards can be prepared with doubles of the counting pattern of fives to 50, or tens to 100.

PROBLEM SOLVING: NUMBERS AND MONEY..........

Activity *Number patterns*

LEARNING OBJECTIVE

Solve simple mathematical problems or puzzles, recognise and predict from simple patterns and relationships. Suggest extensions by asking 'What if ...?' or 'What could I try next?'

Resources

- *Rough paper; pieces of card*

- Call out a number pattern and ask the children what comes next. Here are some examples:

  1, 2, 3, 1, 2, 3, 1, 2, 3 ...

  1, 3, 5, 7, 9, 11, 13 ...

  100, 90, 80, 70 ...

  70, 65, 60, 55 ...

  1, 2, 3, 5, 6, 7, 9, 10, 11, 13, 14, 15 ...

- Write out some descriptions of patterns on pieces of card, for example, 'Counting in threes'. Divide the children into groups. Give each group a piece of rough paper. Hold up a card at a time and give the groups two minutes to work out a number pattern that fits the label.

Watch Points

The second activity might be used to target individuals of different abilities by selecting appropriate number patterns for each child. However, the other children in the class should be involved, by looking on while the pattern is generated, listening to the discussion, and watching and contributing to the recording.

Activity *Tell me another*

LEARNING OBJECTIVES

Solve simple mathematical problems or puzzles, recognise and predict from simple patterns and relationships. Suggest extensions by asking 'What if ...?' or 'What could I try next?' Explain methods and reasoning about numbers orally

- Call out a number and ask an individual child to name another number that 'goes' with it, and to explain why his or her number goes with the first. For example, if 'three' is called, the child may say:

  Four because it is the next counting number.

  Six because it is next in the counting pattern of threes.

  Six because it is double three.

  Thirteen because I have added ten.

  Five because it is the next odd number.

- Ask other children in turn to give another number that follows the pattern. Thus, if the first child said:

  Six because it is double three.

  The next child could say:

  Twelve because it is double the six.

  Then the game can be played so that each successive child has to think of a different way of linking their number to the number called.

Watch Points

If children have difficulties, prompt them as to where they might go next, for example, 'What if you double this number?' 'What do you already know about the number that might help?'

Activity *What does it cost?*

LEARNING OBJECTIVE

Use mental strategies to solve simple problems** set in 'real life', money or measurement contexts **using counting, addition, subtraction, doubling and halving, explaining methods and reasoning orally

- Invent 'number stories' involving the items and children in the class. For example:

  Zak lost his pencils at school. He wondered how much he needed to save to buy five more. They cost 10p each.

  The children can call out the answer or Zak can give the answer himself.

  Extension: give the children a range of number sentences, for example,

  □ + 8 = 10
  20 − 5 = □

  Ask the children to complete the number sentence and to give a number story involving the numbers in 'real life' or money contexts to match it.

Resources

- *Some objects that would only cost a few pence. You could use the same resources as for 'Pocket money' (the following activity) or large cards with pictures showing the objects. Give each object a price orally, or with price cards.*

Watch Points

You could ask the children to make up story problems for others to answer. 'Number stories' are very important in helping to reinforce number facts; they allow children to visualise the story problem involved.

Activity *Pocket money*

LEARNING OBJECTIVES

Recognise coins of different values
Find totals and change from up to 20p
Work out how to pay an exact sum using smaller coins

- Place prices alongside each item. Hold up each one, show what it is, say what it is and say how much it costs. Tell the children they have pocket money. For example, you may begin with 5p pocket money and make the prices of the items less than that. In later sessions the pocket money can be 10p, 15p and 20p.

- Then hold up one or more of the items. Say:

  If you buy this ruler what change will you get from your pocket money?

  Allow the children to call out answers at first.

- Ask questions of groups or individuals, and encourage the others in the class to check the answers.

Resources

- *A comic, a pack of stickers, a pencil, a ruler and an eraser; pieces of card (folded to stand up) on which to write the prices of the items*

Watch Points

In subsequent sessions, it might also be useful to ask how the children will pay for each item. Ask the children to suggest for different combinations of coins.

Activity *Pounds and pence*

LEARNING OBJECTIVE

Recognise all coins and begin to use £.p notation for money

- Ask individual children to respond to challenges you first issue to the whole class. Here are some examples featuring typical prices.

  Which toy costs five pounds sixty?

  Which toy has ninety-nine pence in the price?

  Which toy costs more than the truck?

  Which toy is most expensive?

  Which toys could you buy if you had only three pounds to spend?

  Can you put the toys in order of price?

Resources

- *A collection of toys (which can differ from session to session) set out 'for sale'. Write decimal prices on cards and place them on the toys so the children can see them. You can use STPM Year 2 Shop* ***Posters****.*

Watch Points

You could be the shopkeeper. Ask children to buy things from you and tell you what their change should be. Ask the children to answer your questions using complete sentences.

Activity *Numbers up*

LEARNING OBJECTIVE

Recognise odd and even numbers to at least 30

- Give each child a card (they do not have to be given out in order). Ask the children to hold up their card if the answer to your question is 'yes'. Give some questions that apply to some of the numbers in the set, up to the total in use, such as:

  Is it less than your age?

  Is it more than sixteen?

  Is it odd?

  Is it even?

  Is it a multiple of two?

  Add ten, is the answer twenty or more?

  Extension: the number cards might be extended to include 50 or more.

Resources

- *Cards, numbered from one to the number of children in the class (zero can be included)*

Watch Points

This session can be repeated many times for many different objectives. For example, a session on multiplication facts from the 2, 5 and 10 times tables might include questions such as: 'Is the number more than five times ten?' 'Double it. Is the answer less than twenty?'

Activity *All change*

LEARNING OBJECTIVES

Use mental addition, subtraction, simple multiplication and division to solve simple word problems involving numbers in 'real life' or money, using one or two steps
Explain how the problem was solved
Find totals, give change, and work out which coins to pay

Resources

- *Three 'mystery' parcels wrapped in different coloured paper; cards with prices on (price ranges appropriate to the work being covered)*

Watch Points

Use 'mystery' parcels so that you can assign a range of prices. You could use small toys but the range of 'realistic' prices would then be limited.

- Give each parcel a price label. Place the parcels where they can be seen. Ask the children questions about the parcels. For example:

  How much do the green and red parcels cost in total?

  If I buy the red parcel what change will I have from...? (according to the given price range)

  Which parcel(s) can I buy if I have... ? (limit the sum to allow no more than two parcels to be bought)

  How much will the blue parcel cost if I get it at half price?

- Preface each challenge by selecting who can call out the answer, for example, the whole class, all the boys, all the six-year-olds or target individual children.

Support: limit the prices to numbers and coins with which the children are familiar.

Extension: give the parcels different price labels (involving numbers/coins that reflect the children's experiences) and ask another set of questions. For example:

Which coins could you use to pay for the parcel that costs £5.10?

Activity *Function fun*

LEARNING OBJECTIVES

Solve mathematical problems or puzzles
Extend understanding of the operations of addition and subtraction
Understand the operation of multiplication as repeated addition or describing an array, and begin to understand division as grouping (repeated subtraction) or sharing

- Hold up two number cards. Put these numbers into the function machine. Tell the children that something has happened to the numbers and then lift out an 'output' card with an 'answer' on it. The children should work out what has happened to the numbers and hold up the side of their card showing what they think happened (was the number multiplied, added, divided or subtracted?).

- Here is an example to show how the game works:

  Hold up number cards 5 and 11.

  Here are two numbers. Something is going to happen to them when they go into the function machine. (Place the cards in the box.)

  And out comes 16. What has happened to the numbers?

  (The children fold back and hold up their cards showing the addition sign.)

- Repeat the game with different numbers.

Resources

- *For each child create a card folded over with four maths signs on: plus sign (+) on front, division sign (÷) on the inside left, multiplication sign (×) on inside right and subtraction sign (−) on the back; a card box to use as a function machine; small cards numbered according to the maths you want the children to practise*

Watch Points

You could make the four operations cards using words instead of signs so that the children read and call out the words, thus reinforcing the use of the appropriate mathematical language.

Activity Cash box

LEARNING OBJECTIVES

Use developing mathematical ideas and methods to solve practical problems *involving counting and comparing in real or role play context*
Recognise coins of different values
Work out how to pay an exact sum using smaller coins

- Play the following games in different sessions:
  - Describe a coin and ask the children to point to the correct one on the card.
  - Give the value of the coin and ask the children to point to it.
  - Ask the children which two (or three) coins they could add on the card to make some totals, for example: 15p (10p and 5p), 71p (50p, 20p and 1p).
  - Play equivalence games. For example:

  Five 2p coins make one of these. (The answer is a 10p coin.)

  Support: repeat the activity using coins up to 50p.

  Extension: repeat the activity using a £2 coin.

Resources

- *A card strip with copies of coins from 1p to £1 stuck on in order. You will need enough for the children to have one between two. (Make these, or use STPM Year 1* ***Resources****.)*

Watch Points

Work with real coins, for example, when doing a demonstration, so that the children have the opportunity to look at and handle them.

Activity *Tommy Tall*

LEARNING OBJECTIVE

Use language such as more or less, longer or shorter, heavier or lighter … to compare two quantities, *then more than two, by making direct comparisons of lengths or masses*

Watch Points

Some children may be sensitive about their height. You might prefer to use toys, for example, dolls, for this comparing activity.

- Ask three children to stand in front of the class. Place the flat of a hand above each child's head and remind them that when we measure from the ground to the top of their heads we are measuring height and we say 'How tall?' Ask the class to compare the heights of the children.

- Then give them some quick-fire questions, as follows.

  (In the example questions Sally, Kamran and Sam are in descending order of height.)

  Who is the tallest?

  Who is taller than Kamran?

  Who is shortest?

  Who is shorter than Sally?

  What can we say about Kamran's height?

- These questions can be called out to individual children, groups within the class or the whole class.

Support: you could introduce the activity by standing just two children back to back and comparing their heights using 'taller than' and 'shorter than' to describe the comparisons.

Activity *Long snakes, short snakes*

LEARNING OBJECTIVES

Understand and use the vocabulary related to length
***Compare two lengths by direct comparison**: extend to more than two*

- Invite two children to each choose a snake and hold it up for the class to see. Compare the lengths of the snakes, and then fire some questions at the whole class, such as:

  Which is longer: the pink or the green snake?

  Which is shorter: the blue or the red snake?

- Repeat the activity with different pairs of snakes.
- Then ask children to choose three or more snakes and issue challenges like these:

  Is the pink snake the longest snake?
  Which is the shortest snake?
  Name a snake that is longer than the pink one, but shorter than the red one.

- Then ask individuals to make comparisons, while the class looks on. For example:

  John, can you compare the lengths of the green and red snakes?

Extension: if children have been introduced to standard units of length you might also ask them to make estimates of the lengths of the snakes, for example, 'two and a bit metres'.

Resources

- *Brightly coloured card snakes of a range of lengths. The children could make these.*

Watch Points

In subsequent sessions three or more snakes can be compared, pointing out the shortest and longest. You might also set the problem in a story context, for example, 'The snakes had an argument about which of them was the longest/shortest.'

Activity *Pick the parcel*

LEARNING OBJECTIVES

Understand and use the vocabulary related to mass
***Compare two masses by direct comparison:** extend to more than two*

- Sit the children in a circle, and pass the parcels around so that every child handles each one and can make their own comparisons.
- Then ask the children questions which involve an understanding of these comparisons, such as:

  Is the red parcel lighter than the green one?
  Is the green parcel heavier than the yellow one?
  Find a parcel which is lighter than the blue one.
  Which parcel is heaviest?
  Which parcel is lightest?

Resources

- *Three 'parcels', wrapped in different coloured papers, all the same size, but of markedly different masses. You can make these with three identical boxes with a small blob of Plasticine© or block of wood in one, a larger blob or wooden block in another, and the third one left empty.*

Watch Points

In subsequent sessions, change the masses of the parcels so that the comparisons produce different answers.

Activity *Sand in my bucket*

LEARNING OBJECTIVES

Understand and use the vocabulary related to capacity
***Compare two capacities by direct comparison:** extend to more than two*

- Show the children the buckets and the scoop. Remind children that an estimate is a sensible guess. Ask:

  Estimate how many scoops of sand will fill the buckets.

- After a number of estimates, invite several children to fill the buckets in turn, while the class count out loud the number of scoops taken. Stand the full buckets side by side and ask the children the following questions:

  Which holds most?
  Which holds least?
  Which holds more than …?
  Which holds less than …?

Resources

- *A large sand tray, at least three buckets of different sizes, spades or scoops*

Watch Points

The comparisons can be made more challenging by tipping some of the sand out of the containers or from one to the other, and then asking questions such as, 'Which bucket has more sand than the yellow bucket?'

Activity *Length using non-standard units*

LEARNING OBJECTIVES

Understand and use the vocabulary related to length
Compare two lengths by direct comparison
Measure using uniform non-standard units
Suggest suitable uniform non-standard units and measuring equipment to estimate, then measure a length

- Remind the children of the parts of themselves they can use as measures of length. These include thumbs, hand-spans, cubits, feet, paces and strides.

- Describe some lengths that you would like them to measure, such as:
  - across the room, the carpet, the corridor, the playground or the doorway
  - along the table or bookshelf
  - the length of a book, a pencil or a coat
  - around a pillar or flower bed.

- Ask the children to decide which would be the best unit of measurement to use for each length.

- In subsequent sessions remind the children that they may have used uniform units like ribbon or garden canes to do measuring. Produce the box of resources. Choose three to show the children as the 'measuring units' of the day. Call out things that you want them to measure and ask which of the chosen units would be best for the job.

  Extension: ask the children to suggest a suitable standard unit.

Resources

- *A box of items including the following: a book, a pencil, a matchbox, a piece of string, a skipping rope and a paper clip*

Watch Points

This session checks on children's developing knowledge of non-standard units in order to prepare them for using and measuring using standard units.

Activity *Mass and capacity*

LEARNING OBJECTIVES

Understand and use the vocabulary related to mass and capacity
Compare two masses or capacities by direct comparison
Measure using uniform non-standard units
Suggest suitable uniform non-standard units and measuring equipment to estimate, then measure a mass or capacity

Resources

- *A range of objects with different masses; differently sized containers that can hold sand or water*

- Hold up a selection of items and ask the children to make estimates and comparisons, which they can test out later, such as:

  Which do you think is lighter (of two items)?
  Which do you think is heavier (of two items)?
  Which do you think is lightest (of three or more items)?
  Which do you think is heaviest (of three or more items)?
  Do you think this weighs more or less than the bag of sugar?
  How many mugfuls will fill this jug?

  Extension: ask questions using standard units, such as:
  Which things here do you think weigh a kilogram?
  How many kilograms do you think you weigh?
  Which pan do I need for a litre of water?

Activity *Measuring length*

LEARNING OBJECTIVE

Suggest suitable units and equipment to estimate or measure lengths

- Ask what the children would use to measure things in the room or around school, for example, around the playground, the height of the door, a thumb, around a PE hoop, across the classroom, along the corridor, across the entrance hall.
- Ask a child to come and select the tool they would use. Discuss with the child the reasons for the choice. Ask the child for example, roughly how many metre sticks they think would fit across the hall.

Resources

- *Tools for measuring length. These should include school rules, tape measures, metre sticks, trundle wheels, pocket spring tapes.*

Watch Points

You could include uniform non-standard units and equipment, for example, matchsticks or garden canes.

You might record the class estimates on the board, particularly if you have suggested recording to the nearest metre. You could then refer to this in a future plenary session if/when the practical measuring activity has been completed.

Activity *How heavy, how full?*

LEARNING OBJECTIVE

Estimate, measure and compare masses and capacities, using standard units *(kg, litre)*

- Present a range of the resources available to the children and give them quick-fire challenges. Offer comparisons without units, judgements involving non-standard units and work with standard units. Here are some suggestions:
- Comparisons without units:

  Which do you think is lighter (of two items)?

  Which do you think is heavier (of two items)?

  Which do you think is lightest (of three or more items)?

  Which do you think is heaviest (of three or more items)?

  Do you think this weighs more or less than the bag of sugar?

  Which holds more (of two containers)? Which holds less?

  Which holds most (of three or more containers)? Which holds least?
- Using non-standard units:

  How many of these marbles do you think would weigh the same as this?

  How many mugfuls will fill this jug?
- Using standard units:

  Which things here do you think weigh a kilogram?

  How many kilograms do you think you weigh?

  How much water does a mug hold?

  Which pan do I need for a litre of water?

  How many litre cartons will fill the bucket?

Resources

- *A bag of sugar, a bag of barbecue charcoal, a pack of wadding (used to fill cushions), a bag of potatoes, or other suitable packs where the 'weight' is marked. (Mask any labels saying 'weight' before the lesson.) A milk bottle, a measuring jug, transparent beakers and glasses, an empty litre carton, a pail of water with food colouring added.*

Watch Points

This kind of activity is excellent for the introduction to a lesson, where some of the children go on to have first-hand experiences of similar challenges.

Activity *Solomon Grundy*

LEARNING OBJECTIVES

Understand and use the vocabulary related to time
Order familiar events in time
Know the days of the week

Resources

- *A copy of the rhyme 'Solomon Grundy'*

- Say aloud the 'Solomon Grundy' rhyme:

  Solomon Grundy,
  Born on Monday,
  Christened on Tuesday,
  Married on Wednesday,
  Took ill on Thursday,
  Worse on Friday,
  Died on Saturday,
  Buried on Sunday,
  And that was the end
  Of Solomon Grundy.

- Then ask questions such as:

  Which day comes after Monday?
  Which day follows Wednesday?
  The day before Saturday is Friday. What is the day before that?
  Tuesday is next to Saturday. Is this true?
  Which days are weekend days?
  Which days are weekdays?

Watch Points

An excellent story for sequencing and days of the week work is *The Very Hungry Caterpillar* (Eric Carle, Hamish Hamilton, London, 1969).

Activity *What's the time Mr Wolf?*

LEARNING OBJECTIVES

Understand and use the vocabulary related to time
Read the time to the hour

Resources

- *A large card clock face*

- Set the clock face to something o'clock (for example, two o'clock), while the children call out:

  What's the time Mr Wolf?

  They can then say:

  It is two o'clock.

  Repeat this action several times. Then allow children in turn to take the part of the wolf.

- This activity can be played as a game in the hall. The children stand at one end and the teacher at the other. The children call out the time on the clock and step towards the teacher, using the same number of steps as it is o'clock. When the teacher sets the clock to 12 noon and calls 'Dinner time', the children scuttle away from the 'wolf' who pretends to chase them.

Activity *The house that Jack built*

LEARNING OBJECTIVES

Begin to understand and use the vocabulary related to time
Order familiar events in time
Begin to know the days of the week in order
Begin to read o'clock time

Resources

- *Choose a rhyme or story where there is a sequence of events, and where it is possible to ask questions using words like 'before', 'after' and 'next'. For example, 'This is the House that Jack Built' (see **The Puffin Book of Nursery Rhymes**).*

- **This is the House that Jack Built**

This is the malt
That lay in the house that Jack built.

This is the rat,
That ate the malt
That lay in the house that Jack built.

This is the cat,
That killed the rat,
That ate the malt
That lay in the house that Jack built.

This is the dog,
That worried the cat,
That killed the rat,
That ate the malt
That lay in the house that Jack built.

This is the cow with the crumpled horn,
That tossed the dog,
That worried the cat,
That killed the rat,
That ate the malt
That lay in the house that Jack built.

This is the maiden all forlorn,
That milked the cow with the crumpled horn,
That tossed the dog,
That worried the cat,
That killed the rat,
That ate the malt
That lay in the house that Jack built.

This is the man all tattered and torn,
That kissed the maiden all forlorn,
That milked the cow with the crumpled horn,
That tossed the dog,
That worried the cat,
That killed the rat,
That ate the malt
That lay in the house that Jack built.

This is the priest all shaven and shorn,
That married the man all tattered and torn,
That kissed the maiden all forlorn,
That milked the cow with the crumpled horn,
That tossed the dog,
That worried the cat,
That killed the rat,
That ate the malt
That lay in the house that Jack built.

This is the cock that crowed in the morn,
That waked the priest all shaven and shorn,
That married the man all tattered and torn,
That kissed the maiden all forlorn,
That milked the cow with the crumpled horn,
That tossed the dog,
That worried the cat,
That killed the rat,
That ate the malt
That lay in the house that Jack built.

This is the farmer sowing his corn,
That kept the cock that crowed in the morn,
That waked the priest all shaven and shorn,
That married the man all tattered and torn,
That kissed the maiden all forlorn,
That milked the cow with the crumpled horn,
That tossed the dog,
That worried the cat,
That killed the rat,
That ate the malt
That lay in the house that Jack built.

- Allow the children to recite the rhyme or respond to questions about the story. Phrase the questions so that the children have to answer using words we regard as being part of time vocabulary. Here are some examples that could be used with 'This is the House that Jack Built':

  What came before the cow with the crumpled horn?

  What comes next after the dog that worried the cat?

Watch Points

There are many other examples of children's stories where there is a repeated sequence of events, such as *The Elephant and the Bad Baby* (Elfrida Vipont, Picture Puffins, Penguin Books, Harmondsworth, 1971), 'The Enormous Turnip' and 'The Runaway Pancake'. (If you have STPL in school the latter can be found in the *Big Pink Story Book* and the *Big Blue Story Book (2)* respectively.)

Activity *Days of the week*

LEARNING OBJECTIVES

Understand and use the vocabulary related to time
Order familiar events in time
Know the days of the week

Resources

- *A copy of the song 'The Appleman'*

- **The Appleman**

  Well, well, well,
  Which of you can tell?
  How many apples did the old man sell?
  One on Monday,
  Two on Tuesday,
  Three on Wednesday,
  Four on Thursday,
  Five on Friday,
  Six on Saturday,
  Well, well, well,
  Now can you tell? –
  How many apples did the old man sell?

  Teach the children the song to give them practice in calling out the days Monday to Saturday.

- Seat all the children in a circle. Ask one child to begin with:

  On Monday I ...

  and to invent a mime and say the action.

  The next child begins:

  On Tuesday I ...

  When seven children have had a go, the whole class can recite the rhyme they have created and do the actions. Then begin a new set of actions starting with the next child in the circle. A rhyme may go something like this:

  On Monday I clapped my hands,
  On Tuesday I read a book,
  On Wednesday I washed my hair,
  On Thursday I made a face,
  On Friday I played my recorder,
  On Saturday I caught a ball,
  On Sunday I ate a big lunch.

Activity *Tick tock*

LEARNING OBJECTIVES

Understand and use the vocabulary related to time
Read the time to the hour or half-hour on analogue clocks

Resources

- *Small card clock faces with movable hands (one for every child), a large class clock face, and a large clock face from which the minute hand can be removed*

- Ask the children to set their small clock faces to match 'o'clock' or 'half past' times which you set on the big class clock. Individual children can then say what the time is.

- Call out a time (o'clock or half past) and give the children the opportunity to set their clocks and hold them up to show.

- Set the class clock face at a time (o'clock or half past) and ask the children to set theirs at one hour or one half-hour earlier or later. Then ask questions such as:

  What time is it? (Seven o'clock.)

  Can you set your clocks at one hour earlier than seven o'clock? Don't say the time, just set your clocks and hold them up.

  What time does it say on your clock, Tina?

  Now set your clocks again, making them half an hour later than six o'clock.

- In a separate session, show the children a clock without the minute hand. Explain that the minute hand has fallen off. Ask them whether it is possible to tell 'o'clock' or 'half past' when only the hour hand can be seen.

  Ask them where the hour hand is when a clock says o'clock. Try out the hour hand on the numerals. Point out that when the hand points directly at a number, we know the clock says 'o'clock'. Then place the hour hand halfway between numbers and remind them that in this position, the clock says 'half past'.

  Set the hand at a number and then halfway between numbers, and ask the children what the time is. Do this several times.

Activity *Passing time*

LEARNING OBJECTIVES

Use and begin to read the units of time
Suggest suitable units of time to estimate or measure time

- There are two games that can be played with resources like those listed here. The first relates to 'How long ago?' and the second 'How much time does it take?' Both games involve you offering challenges about these aspects of time. Here are some examples:

  (Holding up the moon picture.) How long ago was it night time? Was it seconds, minutes, hours or days ago?

  (Holding up the ice-cream picture.) How much time do you think it takes to eat an ice-cream? Is it seconds, minutes or hours?

- With the other pictures the challenges might include the following:

  How long ago was it your birthday/Christmas/Diwali?

  When did you last have a new coat/eat an ice-cream/walk the dog/go to the supermarket/play a computer game/see the moon?

  How much time does it take to put on your coat/walk the dog/go to the supermarket/play a computer game?

Resources

- *Cards with pictures of events or things which signal activities. For example, birthday cake, Christmas tree (or other annual religious festivals), a child's coat, ice-cream, dog with lead, supermarket trolley, computer with game on screen, moon. When you have read the ideas for this activity, decide on the subjects that best suit your class.*

Watch Points

The names of the months can feature in the exercise. To help children recall the order, ask them to help invent and then learn a rhyme. It can include special events in your school calendar.

Activity *Time's up*

LEARNING OBJECTIVE

Read the time to the hour, half-hour or quarter hour on an analogue clock and a 12-hour digital clock, and understand the notation 7:30

- Set up a digital time using the numerals and stand. Invite the children to set their clocks to this time. They should then hold up their clocks. Ask them how the digital time is read, and then how it is read from their clocks. Begin with work on the hours (o'clock).
- In subsequent sessions work on half-past and then the quarter hours.

Resources

- *Small card clock faces with movable hands (one for every child); large class clock face; card stand for number flashcards; number cards as follows: two sets of numerals 0–9, one set of numerals 0, 1, 2, and one set of numerals 0–5; card with two dots on it, as they appear between the hours and minutes in a digital array*

Watch Points

In some sessions set the class card clock to a time and then invite a child to set up the matching digital time on the stand. The rest of the class can inspect this and call out both analogue and digital times.

Activity *What's my shape?*

LEARNING OBJECTIVES

Use language such as circle or bigger to describe the shape and size of solids or flat shapes
Begin to name solids such as a cube, cone, sphere and flat shapes such as circle, triangle, square, rectangle …

- Draw a flat shape or stick a picture of solid shape on a piece of card. Cover the shape from view with another piece of card and then slowly reveal it, starting from the top of the card. Ask the children to put their hands up when they think they know what the shape is. Stop revealing the shape when some hands have been raised, and ask individual children for the name of the shape.

  Why do you think the shape is a cube?

  What do you see that tells you this?

- Continue revealing the shape until all the hands have been raised.
- Repeat with different examples.

Resources

- *Card; pictures of solid shapes in the everyday environment, for example, traffic cones, packaging boxes, balls*

Watch Points

This activity can be played over many different sessions with an increasing range of shapes. Encourage the children to use appropriate mathematical vocabulary at all times. For example, 'I can see four corners,' 'The shape has a curved face,' 'The shape is not square'.

Activity *Mystery shapes*

LEARNING OBJECTIVE

Use everyday language to describe features of familiar 2-D and 3-D shapes

- Place either the 3-D or the 2-D shapes inside the bag. Ask the children to sit in a circle. Allow a child to put a hand into the bag and feel one of the shapes. The child should describe it to the class, without saying its name. The children listen. Ask one of them to say what they think the shape is and the reasons for their decision. Ask other children if their answers are different. Finally ask the child to take the mystery shape out of the bag and say its name.

- The game can be played several times over many sessions, with different children choosing a shape each time.

Extension: repeat the activity using other shapes such as a pentagon, a hexagon and an octagon.

Resources

- *A collection of 3-D shapes (cube, cone, sphere, cylinder) and 2-D shapes (circle, triangle, square, rectangle) made of wood or plastic; a 'feely bag', in thick material so the contents of the bag do not show through*

Watch Points

You can reinforce and add to the child's description of the shape, by describing it fully when it has been drawn from the bag. In this activity, therefore, not only will individuals have the chance to handle shapes and use correct mathematical vocabulary, but all the children will be given the chance to listen to it being used by the teacher and other children.

2-D AND 3-D SHAPES

Activity *Describe a shape*

LEARNING OBJECTIVE

Use everyday language to describe features of familiar 3-D shapes

- Hand out the shapes at random to the children. Ask them to hold up their shapes so that the rest of the class can see them. Then ask them to point to the correct shapes as you call out the shape names.

- Take each shape in turn and play the following game. Ask the child holding the shape to say its name and something about it. They should then hand the shape to someone else, who then says the name of the shape and something else about it. This can continue until the children have no more information to add. That shape then goes out of play and another shape is chosen.

Resources

- *Cube, cuboid, pyramid, sphere, cone, cylinder*

Watch Points

You could list the features of each shape under its name on the board as the children identify them.

Activity *2-D shapes*

LEARNING OBJECTIVE

Use everyday language to describe features of familiar 2-D shapes

- Put all the shapes up on the board. Tell the children you are going to choose a shape without saying which shape it is, and that you are going to describe the shape. Ask the children to put their hand up after each piece of information and say what shape it might be.

- Here is an example:

  It has straight sides. (It could be a triangle, square, rectangle, or star.)

  It has four sides. (It could be a square or a rectangle.)

  There are two pairs of sides that match. (It must be a rectangle.)

  Extension: extend the range of shapes to include pentagons, hexagons and octagons.

Resources

- *Large card shapes of a circle, a triangle, a square, a rectangle (you could display STPM shape* ***Posters****)*

Watch Points

When the children are skilled at doing this activity, ask individual children to take turns at choosing and describing the shapes.

Activity *Folded shapes*

LEARNING OBJECTIVES

Use everyday language to describe features of familiar 2-D and 3-D shapes
Fold shapes in half, then make them into symmetrical patterns

- Hold up the cards in turn and ask the children questions.
  What shape is this?
  (Point to one sector.) **How much of the shape is this piece?**
  (Point to another sector.) **How much of the shape is this piece?**
  If it was a cake which piece would you rather have?
- Then, using the fraction card pieces:
  (Point to a sector.) **Eric, please come and find a fraction piece which matches this.**
  What fraction of the whole circle is Eric's piece? (Eric holds his piece up to match the sector on the shape outline.)
- Repeat the activities with the other shapes.

Resources

- *Set of large card shapes (squares, rectangles, triangles, circles hexagons, pentagons) with fraction divisions (halves or quarters) marked on them; card shapes for the fraction parts. For example, if you use a circle divided into quarters, you will also need card shapes of the four fraction shapes of the circle.*

Watch Points

In subsequent sessions children can match two sectors and talk about two quarters of the shapes. Check that children are aware that one half and two quarters are equivalent fractions.

2-D AND 3-D SHAPES

Activity *Thinking shapes*

LEARNING OBJECTIVES

***Use the mathematical names for 3-D shapes**, including the pyramid, cylinder, sphere, cube, cuboid, cone ...*
***Sort shapes and describe some of their properties** such as the number of shapes or faces, and the number of corners*

Resources

- *A cube, cuboid, pyramid, sphere, cone and cylinder*

- Tell the children that you are going to think of a shape, and tell them something about it. They should put up their hands and say which shape they think it is.

  Here is an example:

  I *can only see one of its faces. It is a square.* (It could be a cube, cuboid or square-based pyramid.)

  I *can see another face. That also is a square.* (It could be a cuboid or a cube.)

  The shape has eight corners. (It could be a cuboid or a cube.)

  It has six faces. They are all square. (It is a cube.)

- Try this mystery puzzle for other shapes.

Watch Points

You might use the cube to confirm the answers the children have given.

Activity *Shadow shapes*

LEARNING OBJECTIVE

***Use the mathematical names for 2-D shapes**, including the pentagon, hexagon, octagon ... **describe some of their properties** such as the number of sides and corners*

Resources

- *Card shapes including circle, triangle, square, rectangle, pentagon, hexagon, octagon (these can be regular or irregular), and an overhead projector*

- Lay out one or more shapes on the projector so that the silhouettes are projected onto the screen.

- Issue challenges to the children, such as:

  Eddie, can you tell us about this shape?

  What is this shape called?

  Name two shapes you can see here that are alike in some way.

  What is the shape with most sides called?

Watch Points

For all of these shape activities it would be useful to display flash cards with the words that the children should know and use, for example, 'corner', 'sides', 'faces'.

Activity *Where's the spider?*

LEARNING OBJECTIVE

Use everyday words to describe position, direction and movement

- **Little Miss Muffet**

  Little Miss Muffet,
  She sat on a tuffet,
  Eating her curds and whey;
  Down came a spider,
  And sat down beside her,
  And frightened Miss Muffet away!

- Ask a child to take the part of 'Miss or Master Muffet' and ask the children to say the rhyme while you place the spider 'beside' her or him. After the rhyme discuss what we mean when we say 'beside' her or him. Repeat the rhyme placing the spider on the other side of the child (but still 'beside') at the appropriate moment.

- Choose another '(Miss or Master) Muffet'. Ask the children to look very carefully at where the spider sits this time. Let the children say the rhyme and place the spider in front of her or him. The children should respond by singing:

  Along came a spider and sat down in front of (Miss or Master) Muffet.

  Repeat the rhyme placing the spider behind '(Miss or Master) Muffet'.

Resources

- *Cushion, large soft toy or card spider on elastic; copy of the rhyme 'Little Miss Muffet' (see* ***The Puffin Book of Nursery Rhymes****)*

Watch Points

Do any of the children understand 'beside' as 'next to'?

Allow plenty of children to take a turn, so that the activity covers all of the appropriate positional vocabulary, including 'on', 'over', 'above'. If the child sits on a chair the words 'under' and 'below' can also be included.

Activity *Where is it now?*

LEARNING OBJECTIVE

Use everyday language to describe position, direction and movement

Resources

- *A soft toy, a table, a box*

- Place the toy in a range of positions in relation to the table and the box. Challenge the children each time the toy is moved, so that they use vocabulary such as: 'on top of', 'underneath', 'under', 'over', 'above', 'below', 'beside', 'behind', 'in front of', 'in', 'out', 'inside', 'outside'.
- For example:

  Where is the toy?

  Where am I moving it now?

  Victor, can you come and put the toy in front of the box?

  What word do we use for where the toy is now?

  Anna, move the toy to new position. What is its new position?

Watch Points

You can also ask the children to describe a simple route you take to move the toy from the box to the table. For example, 'The toy turned to the left or the right and then moved forwards to the table.'

Activity *Turning movements*

LEARNING OBJECTIVES

Use everyday words to describe position, direction and movement
Talk about things that turn

Resources

- *Objects or large pictures (stuck on card) of objects that turn, for example, a simple balance, a roundabout, a screw-topped bottle, a lock and key*

- If there is room, ask all the children to stand up. Hold up a picture or object and ask the children to show you how it moves. When they have tried the movement, ask them to sit down and invite several children to describe how they think it moves. Then let everyone have another try at moving to match the movements of the object.
- Try this game for each of the objects.

Watch Points

If there is not room for the children to stand up, they could indicate the movements using their hands in the air. Check that the children are able to recognise and describe turning movements.

Activity *Hokey Cokey*

LEARNING OBJECTIVE

Recognise whole, half and quarter turns, to the left or right, clockwise or anticlockwise

- Ask the children to stand in a circle. Play 'Hokey Cokey'. The call can be changed so that the children are performing turns and using the ideas clockwise and anticlockwise.
- Thus, the rhyme may go as follows:

  Put your LEFT hand in, put your LEFT hand out, in out, in out and shake it all about.

  Do the hokey cokey, and turn CLOCKWISE, that's what it's all about. Oh!

  Make a QUARTER TURN LEFT. Oh!

  Make a QUARTER TURN RIGHT. Oh!

  Make a QUARTER TURN LEFT,

  Knees bend, arms stretch, rah! rah! rah!

  Support: limit the activity to whole or half turns. For example, ask the children to 'Make two whole turns ...'

Resources

- *This game requires lots of room, so the hall or playground may be a good place to work in.*

Watch Points

Children could make up their own versions of 'Hokey Cokey' and call out the new instructions for the others to follow.

Activity *Moving instructions*

LEARNING OBJECTIVES

Use mathematical vocabulary to describe position, direction and movement
Recognise whole, half and quarter turns to the left or right, clockwise or anticlockwise
Give instructions for moving along a route in straight lines and round right-angled corners

- Sit the children in a circle around the track. Choose a child to hold one of the soft toys. Ask another child to give the toy directions for entering the maze, leaving the maze, crossing the maze or reaching the centre, depending on where the toy begins.

Resources

- *Two soft toys. Make a paper or fabric path track to set down on the floor. This should create a simple maze-like effect with right-angled corners as shown in the illustration.*

Watch Points

When the children have played this several times, with different children taking on the roles of toy and caller, set two toys going, and ask two children to give instructions, each in turn, to see if they can make their toy reach the centre first.

Activity *Shape turns*

LEARNING OBJECTIVE

Use one or more shapes to make, describe and continue repeating patterns ...

- Select one set of shapes and give each child one. Hold up your shape and ask the children to hold theirs up so that it matches. The children should turn their shapes so that the shape they hold is in the same orientation in the air. For example, if the shape in use is the triangle, the teacher can hold it so that any side forms the base and is horizontal, or so that any one of the sides points vertically. Check that the children have matched the orientation.
- Then alter the orientation of your triangle and the children should match again. Do this action several times.
- In other sessions choose a different shape to work with.

Support/Extension: you can also use this activity to check on children's understanding of vocabulary relating to straight lines and turning movements. For example, Year 1: 'whole turn', 'half turn', 'slide' and 'roll'; Year 2: 'whole turn', 'half turn', 'quarter turn', 'clockwise', 'anticlockwise', 'to the left and right'.

Resources

- *Card triangles, squares and rectangles (one of each shape for each child and one for the teacher). All the shapes in each set should be similar (thus, if a right-angled triangle is chosen, they should all be right-angled triangles) but they may vary in size. More shape sets may be required in subsequent sessions.*

Watch Points

In subsequent sessions the game can be played with two or even three shapes. The teacher sets the sequence and orientation on a 'fuzzy' board and the children can replicate it by laying the shapes out on their desks.

Speaking and Listening Maths Reception–Year 2: Record Sheet

MATHS SKILLS	DATES		
	INTRODUCTION	CONSOLIDATION	DEVELOPMENT
Say number names in order in familiar contexts (R)			
Count up to 10 everyday objects (R)			
Recognise numerals 0 to 10 (R)			
Compare two numbers, say which is more or less, say a number between them (R)			
Use adding and subtracting vocabulary (R)			
Relate subtraction to 'taking away' (R)			
Relate addition to combining two groups of objects (R)			
Use maths ideas and methods to solve practical problems (R)			
Compare quantities through direct comparisons, and by using containers (R)			
Use everyday words to describe position, direction and movement (R)			
Count in contexts, such as clapping sounds (R)			
Begin to recognise 'none' and 'zero' (R)			
Recite the number names, and count backwards from a number (R)			
Count in tens (R)			
Count in twos (R)			
Find one more/less than a number from 1 to 10 (R)			
Begin to understand and use ordinal numbers (R)			
Order a given set of selected numbers (R)			
Make simple estimates and predictions (R)			
Begin to relate addition to counting on (R)			
Take a small number away from a larger number (R)			
Begin to understand and use the vocabulary of time (R)			
Sequence familiar events (R)			
Begin to know the days of the week in order (R)			
Begin to read o'clock time (R)			
Read and write numerals from 0 to at least 20 (1)			
Count on or back in ones from a small number, and in tens from and back to zero (1)			
Say the number that is 1 or 10 more or less than any number (0–30) (1)			
Use the vocabulary of comparing and ordering numbers (1)			
Order numbers to 20, and position them on a number track (1)			
Understand the operation of addition and subtraction (1)			
Use mental strategies to solve simple problems (1)			
Compare two lengths, masses or capacities by direct comparison (1)			

MATHS SKILLS	DATES		
	INTRODUCTION	CONSOLIDATION	DEVELOPMENT
Use standard or non-standard units to estimate, then measure (1)			
Know the number names in order to 20, from and back to zero (1)			
Count on in twos, and recognise odd and even numbers as 'every other number' (1)			
Count in steps of 5 from zero to 20 or more (1)			
Count on in steps of 3 from zero (1)			
Know what each digit in a two-digit number represents (1)			
Partition two-digit numbers into a multiple of 10 and ones (1)			
Compare two numbers, say which is more or less, say a number between them (1)			
Use the vocabulary of estimation (1)			
Estimate a number of objects that can be checked by counting (1)			
Know addition and subtraction facts for all pairs with a total of 10 (1)			
Recognise that addition can be done in any order (1)			
Do mental calculations by knowing addition can be done in any order (1)			
Add 9 to single-digit numbers by adding 10 then subtracting 1 (1)			
Use patterns of similar calculations (1)			
Use number facts and place value to add or subtract a pair of numbers mentally (1)			
Bridge through 10, then 20, when adding a single-digit number (1)			
Solve maths problems, recognise and predict from patterns/relationships, suggest extensions (1)			
Explain methods and reasoning about numbers orally (1)			
Recognise different coins (1)			
Work out how to pay an exact sum using smaller coins (1)			
Find totals and change from up to 20p (1)			
Use the vocabulary of length, mass and capacity (1)			
Use the vocabulary related to time (1)			
Order familiar events in time (1)			
Know the days of the week and the seasons of the year (1)			
Read the time to the hour or half hour on analogue clocks (1)			
Talk about things that turn (1)			
Use shapes to make, describe and continue patterns (1)			

MATHS SKILLS	DATES		
	INTRODUCTION	CONSOLIDATION	DEVELOPMENT
Count on or back in ones or tens (2)			
Recognise odd and even numbers to at least 30 (2)			
Read and write numbers to 100 (2)			
Know what each digit in a two-digit number represents (2)			
Order numbers to 100, position them on a number line and 100 square (2)			
Do mental calculations by knowing addition can be done in any order (2)			
Understand multiplication as repeated addition, division as grouping or sharing (2)			
Know halving as the inverse of doubling (2)			
Multiplication facts for the 2 and 10 times table (2)			
Estimate, measure and compare lengths, masses and capacities, using standard units (2)			
Use maths vocabulary to describe position, direction and movement (2)			
Say the number names in order to 100, from and back to zero (2)			
Count on in steps of 3, 4 or 5, from and back to zero, from any small number (2)			
Recognise two-digit multiples of 2, 5 or 10 (2)			
Say the number that is 1 or 10 more/less than any two-digit number (2)			
Compare 2 two-digit numbers, say which is more or less, give a number between them (2)			
Use the vocabulary of estimation and approximation (2)			
Round numbers less than 100 to the nearest 10 (2)			
Recognise and find one half and one quarter (2)			
Recognise equivalent fractions (halves and quarters) (2)			
Extend understanding of addition and subtraction (2)			
Know that more than two numbers can be added (2)			
Add three single-digit numbers mentally or three two-digit numbers (2)			
Repeat addition in a different order (2)			
Check with an equivalent calculation (2)			
Know all pairs of numbers with a total of 20 (2)			
Know all pairs of multiples of 10 with a total of 100 (2)			
Find a small difference by counting up (2)			
Use patterns of similar calculations (2)			
Understand division as sharing equally (2)			
Doubles of all numbers to 10 and the corresponding halves (2)			

MATHS SKILLS	DATES		
	INTRODUCTION	CONSOLIDATION	DEVELOPMENT
Use number facts and place value to do multiplications and divisions mentally (2)			
Know multiplication facts for the 5 times table (2)			
Recognise all coins and use £.p notation (2)			
Use mental addition, subtraction, multiplication and division to do problems using one or two steps (2)			
Find totals, give change, and work out which coins to pay (2)			
Solve maths problems or puzzles (2)			
Use the vocabulary related to time (2)			
Suggest units of time to estimate or measure time (2)			
Read time to hour, half-hour, quarter hour on an analogue clock and 12-hour digital clock (2)			
Recognise whole, half, quarter turns, to left, right, clockwise, anticlockwise (2)			
Give instructions for a route in straight lines and round right-angled corners (2)			

Key

(R) Skill based on Reception Year learning objective.
(1) Skill based on Year 1 learning objective.
(2) Skill based on Year 2 learning objective.
Key objectives are highlighted in **bold**.
This sheet can be photocopied and completed to provide a record for each class or individual child.